THE
WINSTON
CUP

THE WINSTON CUP

DUANE FALK

MetroBooks

MetroBooks

An Imprint of Friedman/Fairfax Publishers

Library of Congress Cataloging-in-Publication Data

Falk, Duane.
   The Winston Cup / Duane Falk.
      p.   cm.
   Includes bibliographical references (p.) and index.
   ISBN 1-56799-834-8
   1. Stock car racing–United States–History. 2. Winston Cup-History.   I. Title.
GV1029.9.S74F35 1999
796.72'0973–dc21   99-23676
                                                       CIP

Editor: Nathaniel Marunas
Art Director: Jeff Batzli
Designer: Kevin Ullrich
Photography Editor: Chris Toliver
Production Manager: Camille Lee

Color separations by Radstock Repro.
Printed in England by Butler & Tanner Ltd.

10 9 8 7 6 5 4 3 2 1

For bulk purchases and special sales, please contact:
Friedman/Fairfax Publishers
Attention: Sales Department
15 West 26th Street
New York, NY 10010
212/685-6610 FAX 212/685-1307

Visit our website:
www.metrobooks.com

Contents

Introduction:
The Origins of Stock Car Racing

The roots of NASCAR are as humble as the small farms and towns of the Southeast that nurtured it. Stock car racing came out of rural Virginia and the Carolinas, where a generation of independent, self-reliant men found relief from labor on the farm or at the cotton mills in the purr of a finely tuned engine or the thrill of speed as they rocketed down dirt lanes. The mechanical skills needed to keep a farm's tractor or truck in good working order were similar to those needed to make the cars faster.

In some cases this aptitude was put to more practical uses than building a hot rod as relief from the tedium of a day job. While football and baseball were devised as pastimes, stock car racing grew, at least in part, out of a very serious profession. The business of making moonshine whiskey had been going on since Colonial times. With the advent of Prohibition in the 1920s, backyard and backwoods stills became the only sources of liquor in a time of soaring demand. Even after the repeal of Prohibition in the early 1930s, homemade 'shine remained a popular—and cheaper—alternative to store-bought liquor. Of course, one reason it was cheaper was that its purveyors neglected to pay taxes on sales, which made it illegal. The government took exception to this application of free enterprise, and local sheriffs and federal revenue collectors, or "revenuers," had full-time jobs tracking down and dismantling stills. As quickly as the stills were broken down, new ones were set up in better-concealed or more remote locations. This left the entrepreneurs with the problem of how to get their product to the consumers. That's where the men with fast cars came in.

Transporting white lightning was by no means a leisure activity—it was deadly serious business. The cars used by these men were carefully crafted to give them the edge they needed to evade or outrun pursuit. Custom suspensions and beefed-up engines on 1930s Fords were de rigueur. Besides often having better equipment than the revenuers, the drivers also developed the split-second reflexes and high-speed driving skills needed to run a country road at night, at top speed, without lights.

Human nature being what it is, it was inevitable that sooner or later someone would claim to have the fastest car or be the most daring driver, and be challenged to prove it. In many places, drag races were run to settle the issue. In the southeastern United States, driving was often as much a battle of wits, nerve, and skill as it was a demonstration of technical superiority, so competition took a different turn.

All over the South, cornfields were cleared and rough circles or ovals plowed into the red earth. Drivers brought their souped-up family cars or hot rods or moonshine cars to the local tracks on Saturday night to compete against one another in rough-and-tumble racing, usually driving their cars to the track, racing them, then driving them (or what was left of them) back home afterward.

These races were almost entirely a grass-roots phenomenon. Tracks were built and run by the owner of the land they sat on, or in some cases by local, small-scale entrepreneurs whose tracks stood out because they had guardrails or stands. The sport gained further momentum in the 1940s, when the incentive for moonshining diminished and former delivery drivers turned their attention to racing instead.

Although there was more opportunity to race, and more fans were gathering to watch the fender-banging at tracks like North Wilkesboro, Hickory, and Asheville, the sport was entirely without leadership or organization. Each track set its own rules, and to collect their winnings competitors often had to rely as much on their skill at chasing down a shifty promoter or at fistfighting as they did on their racing ability. The situation was ripe for change.

Daytona Is the Place

Change came in the form of a racer from the Washington, D.C., area by the name of "Big Bill" France. France and his family relocated to Florida in 1934—stopping at Daytona on their way to Miami to take in the sights of the famous beach where many land speed records had been set over the years. They never left. In that locale, which was already steeped in racing history, France proceeded to write a few pages of history himself.

Through the 1930s, the town of Daytona had made a number of attempts to run races on the beach, but these had met with limited success, and city officials were prepared to throw in the towel. France, a competitor in many of those races, realized the potential in racing and stepped

in as a promoter and organizer. Following the hiatus imposed on all forms of auto racing by World War II, France picked up where he had left off. Realizing that the key to success was a national sanctioning body, an approved schedule of events, and a single set of rules, France brought together a collection of racing insiders for the now-famous 1947 meeting at the Streamline Hotel in Daytona Beach.

One of France's crucial points was that the "stock" in stock car racing must be well defined. For competition to be close, all cars must be roughly equivalent. Furthermore, officials could more easily enforce a set of rules that clearly

The real birthplace of NASCAR was on the sands of Daytona Beach. The race course, used from 1936 until 1958, ran both on the sands and on the road parallel to the beach—Highway A-1-A. Tim Flock crossed the finish line first in this 1954 race, but he was disqualified for illegal engine modifications and Lee Petty got the trophy.

laid out what modifications were acceptable; such rules would also minimize cheating and help to avoid the frequent—and frequently physical—postrace discussions about the legitimacy of a given win.

France wasn't just a good organizer—his experience as a race promoter had taught him that success depends on reading your audience right and playing to them. He saw that the popularity of stock car racing was in large part due to the fans identifying the cars they saw on the track with the cars they drove to and from the track. The southern fans drove Ford and Chevy sedans and had little interest in European or exotic sports cars, so the Strictly Stock division would be based on the popular brands of American cars. The group of organizers at the historic meeting at the Streamline put together two other divisions as well—Modified Stock and Roadsters.

The Birth of NASCAR

The outcome of the 1947 meeting was the formation of the National Association for Stock Car Automobile Racing, or NASCAR. The group had originally come up with the name National Stock Car Racing Association, but the acronym NSCRA was already in use by another organization. Mechanic and racer Jerome "Red" Vogt suggested the now-famous alternative.

While France's vision was most closely tied to the Strictly Stock division, reality dictated a slightly different course for NASCAR's first season in 1948. Detroit was still trying to catch up with the demand for sedans following World War II, and there weren't enough stock cars available. Thus in its first year NASCAR put its efforts behind the Modified Stock division—based on the prewar Ford coupes that had often been the cars of choice for the old moonshine runners. By 1949, though, the Strictly Stock division was ready to roll, and NASCAR's Grand National series began in earnest.

From Dirt Tracks to Superspeedways

The Strictly Stock division (the name soon changed to the Grand National division to give it a more prestigious sound) meant just that. In contrast to all other racing series, these vehicles had to be passenger cars available from the showroom with the bumpers, fenders, and bodywork attached and no mechanical alterations. Those rules were soon challenged—in the very first race.

Given France's background, it is perhaps surprising that the series didn't begin with a race at Daytona Beach.

Instead, the first race was deliberately held at Charlotte Speedway in North Carolina, a 3/4-mile (1.2km) dirt track. Before it had fairly got started, NASCAR itself was challenged. Bruton Smith, director of rival organization NSCRA (which acronym was denied to France), was trying to recruit many of the same racers as NASCAR was. France met NSCRA's threat head-on by scheduling the first full Strictly Stock event in Smith's backyard.

Thirty-three cars ran the 150-mile (240km) event, and some of the drivers' names would echo through NASCAR history—names like Buck Baker, Herb Thomas, and Lee Petty. The apparent winner, Glenn Dunnaway, driving the #25 Ford, was found to have spread rear springs (used by moonshiners to improve the stability of their cars), a clear violation of the NASCAR rules. Dunnaway was disqualified, and Jim Roper, though several laps down, was awarded the win.

The 1949 Strictly Stock season was by no means smooth sailing. By the end of the year, though, eight points races had been run, points standings were compiled, and a champion, Robert "Red" Byron, was declared. The fact that there had been six different winners in the eight events clearly demonstrated that NASCAR's standards had successfully made for close competition. The sport was on its feet and ready to start toddling.

NASCAR's First Ten Years

The 1950s were a decade of growth and fine-tuning for the fledgling organization. It expanded beyond the narrow geographical limits of the Southeast, running races from Connecticut to California. Included among the myriad sponsored tracks was a half-mile (0.8km) dirt track in Heidelberg, Pennsylvania, not far from Pittsburgh (where this author first heard the thunder of race cars and developed a love for the sport).

The typical venues were changing as well. More tracks were being paved, and soon the first superspeedway race was held at South Carolina's new Darlington Raceway. The 1950 Southern 500 featured seventy-five cars racing three wide on a 1.25-mile (2km) paved track. Today, 500-mile (800km) races are the norm and fit nicely into a Sunday afternoon, but at the speeds of the day, that first 500-miler took more than six hours to complete. Nowadays, every fan knows the importance of tires, but at the time only Johnny Mantz, a California native with Indy car experience, realized what would happen to the tires during a race that long on asphalt. Mantz used hard compound tires and drove away from the competition, winning by nine laps.

By the late 1950s, the focus of NASCAR was squarely on its stock division. The modified cars remained popular at tracks that were unable to draw a Grand National event, but stock cars were its bread and butter. Before coming to that conclusion, however, NASCAR made one other foray into a specialty stock segment: the convertible class. In 1956, NASCAR merged with a midwestern organization that featured convertibles. The advantage of the convertibles was that fans were able to get a good look at their favorite drivers "at work in the office." While the convertibles ran their own races, they ran under the same rules as the Grand National division, on the same tracks, with the same drivers, and often on the same day as GN events. In large part because of this overlap, the convertibles class failed to distinguish itself and was discontinued after the 1959 season.

"Madman" Johnny Mantz started the first Southern 500 halfway back in the seventy-five-car field. In only his third NASCAR race he was no one's favorite to win. By lap 50, though, he had taken his Plymouth to the point and stayed there for the only win of his brief career.

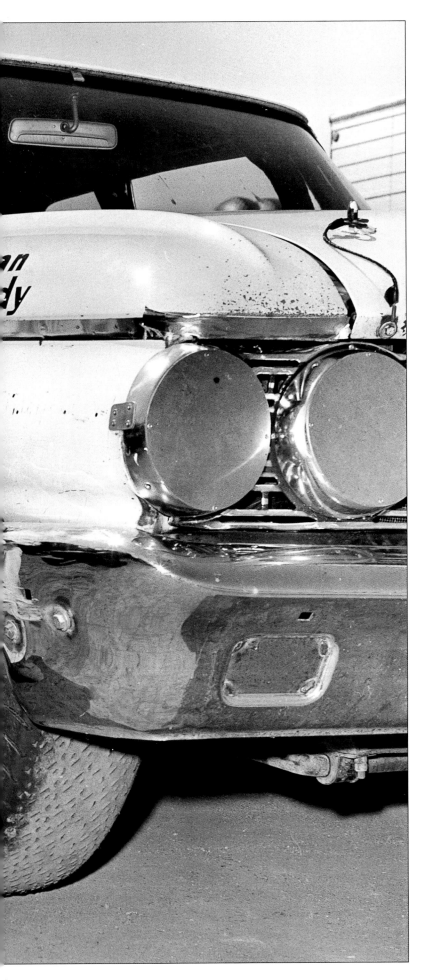

Going Steady with Motor City

The fifties saw the first round of an on-again, off-again relationship between NASCAR and the Detroit auto industry. As NASCAR stabilized and grew, the car manufacturers, realizing the benefit of "Win on Sunday, Sell on Monday," started looking for ways to make their brands more competitive. Since NASCAR was strictly stock, this meant introducing new models and new technology as options on production models. In turn, race teams benefited from the better and faster cars, which in many cases the factories donated to the teams. The relationship cooled, however, when the safety of auto racing came under fire in the late 1950s. At issue was the safety of the spectators, rather than that of the drivers: in 1955, a fiery crash at the 24 Hours of Le Mans had sent a car spinning into the crowd, killing more than a hundred onlookers and drawing fire on all forms of the sport. Mindful of this negative attention and under pressure to focus on consumer aspects of automobile production rather than on speed, the auto manufacturers backed away from the sport, withdrawing their sponsorship and leaving the teams to fend for themselves once again.

Stock Car Racing Is Here to Stay

NASCAR has always been fortunate that at crucial times in its history larger-than-life figures have stepped up to carry the sport forward. When it could easily have stalled at the end of the 1950s, two factors provided the impetus to keep the sport moving and take the organization to a higher level of recognition and success.

Rather than allow the factory withdrawals to stall NASCAR's progress, Bill France again proved his mettle, creating a racing venue that would demonstrate to the world that the sport was here to stay. Even today, the universal reaction of drivers upon entering the Daytona International Speedway for the first time is to stop in their tracks in awe. Imagine how this 2.5-mile (4km) track, with its expanse of infield and wide asphalt racing surface, must have looked to drivers who in 1959 still did most of their racing on small dirt tracks. Daytona was the "house that France built," a speed palace with a vast, sweeping track, plenty of banking to keep the speeds up, and a curved

Back in the old days, the driver did everything. Here Fred Lorenzen checks tire pressure on his #0 Ford before the 1962 World 600.

front stretch to provide better viewing for the fans. Even today, Daytona's design is the model for state-of-the-art racetracks like California Speedway.

The first race at the new Daytona track was everything France could have wanted—and that NASCAR needed. Skeptics questioned whether the drivers and cars could run safely at the speeds the track made possible, but the close competition in the first race dissolved all doubts. As the checkered flag flew, three cars passed the finish line dead even. It turned out that one driver was more than a lap down, but it took three days of reviewing press and fan photos to determine which of the other two—Johnny Beauchamp or Lee Petty—was the winner. The trophy ultimately went to Petty.

The Big Time

Racing on this scale was hard for anyone to ignore or downplay. No longer was NASCAR just a bunch of good ol' boys bangin' their way around rutted dirt tracks. The speed, action, and attendance at the Daytona 500 brought the Grand National racers a new degree of respectability.

And what about those good ol' boys? Tough, no-nonsense drivers characterized the first decade of NASCAR. Lee Petty, Curtis Turner, Buck Baker, the Flock boys—these were drivers who could take inferior equipment and race the wheels off of it. It's interesting to speculate how a driver like Curtis Turner would stack up against today's stars, driving cars that could reliably hold up for more than 100 miles (160km) under the pace he'd set. For some drivers, the no-nonsense attitude applied only when they were on the track. Off-track, many of the headliners of the day were hard-drinking partygoers—not the kind of personalities that made for broad appeal, or good publicity, nationwide.

Superstars on the Superspeedways

The second factor that kept NASCAR on track was the infusion, in its second decade, of a new generation of drivers. Glenn "Fireball" Roberts (so named because of his blazing fastball as a college baseball pitcher) won fame, and hordes of fans, with a string of victories in 1958. Roberts drove his #22 Ford to six wins—including an amazing five in a row—out of only ten starts that year. Perhaps the first popular hero in NASCAR, he gave fans someone to cheer for at a time when NASCAR desperately needed positive attention to offset the sport's roughneck image and help expand its appeal. Roberts was quiet and a

Certainly the most famous second-generation driver, Richard Petty followed his father, Lee, into NASCAR in 1958. The twenty-two-year-old hadn't started accumulating any of his 200 wins by the time this photograph was taken in 1959, but the trademark smile is already in place. 1959 was the year Petty began using the number 43 on his cars.

bit of a loner, but he sure drove a mean race—it was a combination that really appealed to the fans.

There were other fresh faces on the scene as well. Richard Petty was a second-generation driver. A lanky young man with a wide, ready smile, Richard was a sharp contrast to his down-to-business father, Lee. When father and son raced as competitors, Lee clearly cut Richard no slack on the track, to the point of contesting Richard's first apparent victory. (NASCAR agreed and awarded the victory to Lee.) There's one story, perhaps apocryphal, that illustrates the degree of the elder Petty's focus on winning races, a determination he instilled in his son. They say that on one pit stop, Lee, in a hurry to get back to the track, took off with his son, who had been cleaning the windshield, still leaning over the front of the car. He reputedly drove a full lap on the track with Richard hanging on for dear life before he relented and pitted again so his son could disembark.

Another newcomer, Fred Lorenzen, a stylishly good-looking young Californian, was an outsider to the southern racing community, but his polished driving style brought a new attitude and professionalism to NASCAR.

A Decade of Turmoil

By the end of the 1950s, NASCAR, with Bill France at the helm, had proved to be a viable enterprise, capable of meeting and overcoming any number of different challenges. Its strong leadership remained intact, forging a vision for the brave new decade of the 1960s. In fact, France's influence over NASCAR consolidated further as he acquired all but ten shares of NASCAR stock from the original partners by 1963. This made France the final arbiter and sole authority for the organization.

It would take all of the control Bill France could muster to get through the next decade. The 1960s were

Back on the track after a forced four-year hiatus, Curtis Turner hooked up with the Wood Brothers for the 1966 Daytona 500 and a handful of other races that year. Turner had to drop out of the race after only 122 laps because of a broken windshield—one of several drivers to suffer that problem. Richard Petty took the race—his second Daytona win.

a time of tremendous growth for the sport, but also of upheaval, direct contention of France's leadership, and personal tragedy and sorrow.

The Return of Detroit

The central theme of the decade was NASCAR's relationship with the Detroit auto manufacturers. Since 1957, the car makers had participated in the ban on manufacturer involvement in motorsports prompted by safety concerns. Officially, all the majors had washed their hands of auto racing, but for some it was more lip service than company policy. GM, seeing the opportunity to wrest dominance on the track from rival Ford, leaked parts for Oldsmobiles, Chevys, and especially Pontiacs to the teams. Semon "Bunkie" Knudsen, the top man at Pontiac, realized that the potential growth from NASCAR publicity was well worth the risk of finessing the terms of the racing ban.

The inaugural Daytona 500 proved to be too much for any of the factories to ignore, and Ford (like GM) began unofficially providing support. Part of the company's change of heart was due to a change of leadership. Lee Iacocca, the new CEO, realized that NASCAR gave Ford a medium to sell a new image to young buyers. Even Chrysler (Plymouth) returned to the sport, with up-and-coming superstar Richard Petty as their champion. Although by 1960 most of the factories were again involved with racing, the motorsports ban lingered in

the background and would resurface as a factor before the end of the following decade.

Power on the Tracks

With factory involvement back in full force, the phrase that paid was "more power." Detroit stretched the definition of production runs so that NASCAR teams could use bigger and bigger engines and still stay within the confines of the stock rules. The cubic inches of engine displacement were flaunted on the hoods of the cars, and engine size and power were on the rise. In the early 1960s, Pontiac used its headstart on the competition to good advantage, winning almost half of the races in 1961 and 1962.

While factory involvement and competition brought new lifeblood to NASCAR, it came with a high price tag. This was business—big business—and the manufacturers wanted to make sure that their investments panned out. As a result, NASCAR and France found themselves under constant assault as the auto companies petitioned, bargained, and bullied for rules changes and concessions. Wanting to keep all of the majors in the field, France often allowed rules to be bent, sometimes blatantly. This meant that enforcement of the "strictly stock" principle was inconsistent at best.

The house of cards started falling when the Chevy team of Ray Fox and Junior Johnson came to race in 1963 with a new engine that cranked out appreciably higher power than the competition. Though the production status of the "Mystery Motor" was in question (a Ford team owner found out firsthand that Chevy dealerships knew nothing about the new power plant), NASCAR allowed it to run in Daytona's speedweeks. The resulting furor in the motorsports press and among fans had serious repercussions. GM execs, still officially observing the motorsports ban, pulled all backing from race teams, which left the GM teams up in the air, and the rest scrambling for Ford or Chrysler rides. In 1963, Ford was back on top, scoring wins at more than half of the year's events.

Plymouth fought back in 1964 with the powerful Hemi racing engine. This meant another crisis of conscience for France, since the Hemi came nowhere near the production numbers required by the rule book. Even so, the Hemi was allowed to race, in order to keep Mopar involved, and the engine helped Richard Petty capture his first Grand National championship that year. Petty and Chrysler were looking for a repeat in 1965, but France adjusted the rules in response to protests from other teams seeking to curtail the Hemi's (somewhat unfair) dominance.

Rather than accept the handicap, Chrysler, and the top drivers depending on its backing, went elsewhere to race: Richard Petty went drag racing, while others moved to the United States Automobile Club (USAC). Despite all of his machinations, France found himself running a series dominated by one make. In response, he compromised on the Hemi, allowing it on certain speedways in certain car models. Petty and Plymouth returned, and the turbulent 1965 season finally wound to a finish. It was ironic, given the furor of the season, that the championship was won by the easygoing "Gentleman" Ned Jarrett.

The factory controversy would continue through the decade. Cars were now highly specialized, aerodynamic rockets. In some cases, a minimum run of production models was rolled out just to satisfy the NASCAR requirements. The sleek, carefully designed shapes of Cyclones, Torinos, and Superbirds cut through the air, maximizing the speeds gained from the racing engines. The manufac-

No, not drafting, just close racing. Two rag-tops battle it out in NASCAR's last convertible race. Although the convertible division had folded in 1959, Darlington Raceway kept the cars in the spring Revel 300 through 1962, awarding the points within the Grand National Division. Buck Baker's #87 may be following Lee Reitzer in this shot, but Baker finished well ahead of Reitzer in the race.

turers resisted all of NASCAR's attempts to keep extravagance in check, and the decade ended much as it had started: by the end of the 1970 season, Chrysler had severely cut back team support and, with another change in leadership, Ford pulled out of racing altogether. It looked as if the roller coaster ride of factory support had finally come to an end.

Power at the Conference Table

The trials of factory sponsorship were not the only issues that NASCAR faced in the 1960s. There were two serious challenges to Bill France's position as sole authority for the group.

In 1961, Curtis Turner partnered with promoter Bruton Smith to build his own version of the immensely successful Daytona speedway. To meet the construction costs for the Charlotte Motor Speedway, Turner went to the teamsters union for a loan. In return for its support, the union asked Turner to organize the NASCAR drivers. Working with fellow racer Tim Flock, Turner signed on a number of well-known drivers, until Bill France got wind of it and put his foot down. The ultimatum—no union driver would race at any NASCAR-sanctioned track—

Serious faces in the Holman-Moody garage. H&M team members Fred Lorenzen (center) and Nelson Stacy (right) confer with chief mechanic Ralph Moody (left) after the sleek fastback Fords they brought to the 1962 World 600 were ruled illegal. The team switched to backup cars (set up for dirt track racing) and still managed a great showing. Stacy won the race and Lorenzen finished third.

effectively ended Turner's organizing effort. France took the issue further—he banished Turner and Flock from NASCAR for life. In Turner's case, his exile was temporary: in 1966, when France needed name drivers to offset Ford's pullout, he allowed Turner to return. Flock never raced again.

A more serious—and somewhat more successful—attempt to lobby for better conditions for drivers was led by Richard Petty in 1968 with the formation of the Professional Drivers Association (PDA). The 1960s had been a dangerous decade for drivers. With speeds approaching 200 mph (322kph) at France's new Talladega superspeedway in 1969, many drivers were concerned that the cars and tires would not hold up. Though France downplayed the drivers' concerns, even making a show of taking a car around the track himself to demonstrate its safety, the tire manufacturers agreed with the drivers and asked for a speed limit on the race. Most of the GN drivers walked away from the event, leaving a field of drivers mostly from other series. Though membership in the PDA dwindled after the protest (and the organization folded in 1973 after Richard Petty's withdrawal), the confrontation resulted in improved tire formulations and better money for drivers.

The names and faces of NASCAR changed considerably through the 1960s. Richard Petty came to the forefront as a true champion. Drivers like Cale Yarborough, David Pearson, and Bobby Allison started making their mark, forming the nucleus of the top-drawer competition for the next decade and beyond. Crossovers from other, more prestigious racing circuits also helped to polish NASCAR's image. Indy winner Parnelli Jones tried his hand at stock car racing, and Dan Gurney won five events at the Riverside road course. The most famous American racers of all, A.J. Foyt and Mario Andretti, raced in NASCAR throughout the 1960s, and Foyt continued his involvement with stock car racing as a driver and owner well into the 1990s.

The Price of Safety

By the end of the 1970 season, many beloved faces were missing from the field. Although NASCAR has always been progressive about safety improvements, those changes sometimes came in reaction to driver injuries or deaths. The decade started off on a sad note as the racing career of three-time champion and NASCAR "charter member" Lee Petty ended in 1961. A tangle with Johnny Beauchamp in a Daytona qualifying race sent both cars flying over the guardrail in turn four and down an embankment outside the track. Petty suffered critical injuries that, though he

Spectators said it looked like an "ordinary wreck" when Joe Weatherly's Mercury hit a glancing blow to the wall coming out of turn six at Riverside in 1964, but the impact was enough to take the life of the forty-one-year-old Norfolk, Virginia, veteran and defending Grand National champion.

recovered and made a brief comeback, effectively ended his racing career. Beauchamp was also injured and never raced again.

The year 1964 was especially difficult for NASCAR. Besides the problems of factory sponsorship, 1964 saw the loss of several of NASCAR's favorite sons. At the beginning of the year "Little" Joe Weatherly, a practical joker and tough driver in the mold of his buddy Curtis Turner, hit a guardrail at Riverside on the driver's side of the car. Weatherly never wore a shoulder strap, and window nets were not yet standard, so the collision crushed Weatherly's head against the wall, killing him.

Just months later, the sport suffered a second hard blow when hero Fireball Roberts crashed into an opening in the wall at Charlotte, splitting open his fuel tank and setting the car ablaze. Fellow driver Ned Jarrett pulled Roberts from the flames, but Fireball's burns were extensive and he died of the injuries several weeks later.

As car speeds increased, pushing the limits of what tires could take, tire-testing sessions sometimes took on the feel—and the risks—of jet plane test piloting. Two drivers were lost this way in 1964 and 1965. At Charlotte in 1964, Jimmy Pardue was killed when his Pontiac spun out of control at speeds well above the track record, leaving the track and tumbling down an embankment. At the beginning of the 1965 season, a young driver, Billy Wade, likewise lost his life when a tire blew at Daytona.

Retirements also thinned the ranks of NASCAR stars. Ned Jarrett, Marvin Panch, and fan favorite Fred Lorenzen all hung up their helmets during the 1960s.

Another Crossroads

At the end of the decade, NASCAR once again found itself at a turning point. The double-edged sword of factory sponsorship had carried the sport this far, fueled by and fueling the growth of superspeedways and racing heroes. Despite France's best efforts and continued compromises, the well of factory support had run dry for all but a very few teams. The majority of race teams would have to work on shoestring budgets and field older or lower-quality equipment.

The number of fans in attendance was directly proportional to the speeds and competitiveness on display, so a decline in either of the latter could trigger a downward spiral in revenue. Two scenarios seemed likely: either a division of the field into two classes—the one or two remaining factory teams versus everyone else running for second place—or a general stagnation. Either option spelled disaster.

Unlike the previous rounds of factory cutbacks, this one was pretty much across the board, and there didn't appear to be any quick or easy solution. NASCAR clearly needed sponsorship funds, so it was time to look elsewhere for help. Could France again throw a last-minute TD? By spring 1970, the Hail Mary pass was in the air.

No one doubted that Chrylser had the speed, but would they be allowed to use it on the Grand National circuit? Lee Roy Yarbrough (behind the wheel) and Ray Fox (standing) used a supercharged Dodge to set a new closed-course speed record of 181.818 mph (291kph) in 1965 at Daytona. New rules set by NASCAR seemed to penalize Chrysler teams. Fox switched to Chevys for the year but couldn't make them competitive.

Chapter One

The Beginnings of the Winston Cup: 1971 to 1974

The beginning of the 1970s was a tough time for tobacco companies. In the previous decade, scientists had established that the use of tobacco products, especially cigarettes, could have adverse health effects. The link to lung cancer and heart disease led to government regulations in 1966 requiring tobacco manufacturers to put health warnings on packs and cartons of cigarettes. By 1970, legislation was in the works to eliminate all advertising of tobacco products on radio and television. For the first time since cigarette smoking had become popular in America in the late 1800s, it was no longer viewed as a stylish, innocent pleasure. With the writing on the wall for marketing in the United States, major tobacco companies were looking for a new advertising medium.

About the same time, Junior Johnson was out beating the bushes in search of a sponsor for his race team. When the Ford factory withdrew from NASCAR, Johnson's was one of the teams left hanging, and he needed backing to remain competitive. Through Ralph Seagraves, an old buddy and a salesman for the R.J. Reynolds tobacco company, Johnson contacted the company and went to their Winston-Salem headquarters to convince them to sponsor his team.

The company turned down Johnson's request for funding that day, but not because they were unwilling to be involved in racing—far from it. Executives from the company who had recently traveled to Europe to investigate marketing opportunities had seen prominent tobacco advertisements at motorsport and other sports venues. RJR had a big advertising budget, though, and needed a more comprehensive approach than putting their name on the panels of one race team's cars. Johnson recommended that they get in touch with Bill France about series sponsorship options. France and Johnson set up a meeting for the spring of 1970 with Reynolds marketing executives Bob Rechholtz and Art Weber and with Bill Smith, RJR's chairman of the board, to present a proposal for RJR involvement with NASCAR.

Before the meeting, Weber had already taken advantage of an opportunity to attend the Daytona 500, where he had been overwhelmed by the advertising and promotional possibilities. Besides the tremendous number of fans reached directly at the races (the number had climbed to nearly 900,000 for the season by then), the major television networks were beginning to dabble in covering

NASCAR races. This is what clinched it for Weber. While the tobacco companies were forbidden to advertise directly on TV, there were no restrictions on broadcasts of sporting events prominently featuring their brands.

In their March meeting with France, RJR committed to sponsoring the entire NASCAR Grand National series. Starting in 1971, the series would be known as the Winston Grand National, after RJR's top brand. Reynolds would fund the series in a variety of ways. They would establish a points fund—the Winston Cup—to reward drivers for participating in the races. The fund was on a sliding scale, paying more to drivers the higher they finished in the point standings. RJR would also directly sponsor a race—the Winston 500, at France's newest superspeedway, Talladega. The money they proposed putting into the event would ensure a first-class production. The lavish purse would attract a strong field with all of the top teams, which would in turn attract fans, who would attract the television networks, and so on. The sponsored events would of course prominently feature RJR advertising, but the company also carried out an active promotional campaign for the races. Billboards and newspaper and magazine ads were purchased, and Reynolds conducted retail promotions of their products tied to NASCAR.

And the investment was not limited to this initial campaign. It became clear over the first several years of RJR involvement that a number of major tracks were still having trouble drawing enough spectators to make ends meet. Reynolds stepped up their commitment and increased their promotional activities to help bring in the fans. From 1971 to 1975, audiences more than doubled—from 900,000 to more than 2 million—at least in part because of the events' increased exposure, achieved with Reynolds' assistance. The points fund increased significantly from year to year and continues to rise today. Reynolds also started sponsoring special events, including the championship awards ceremony and, of course, the famous Winston Million programs.

Presented with this golden opportunity, France was careful not to put himself in the position of juggling competing sponsors, as he had done during the days of factory sponsorship. And having seen the trouble that USAC had run into when it allowed a second cigarette company to sponsor teams in competition with L&M, its primary series backer, France ruled that no other tobacco company would be allowed to align itself with NASCAR. NASCAR and Reynolds also showed prudence in their approach to Winston advertising and promotion. Although motorsports sponsorship was an advertising area still open to the tobacco companies, they decided it was best to show restraint given the pressures of the time. Although Winston was clearly identified at the tracks as the series sponsor, TV audiences would not see garish billboards for the cigarettes ringing the asphalt. Even the size of the Winston decals on the cars was limited to help avoid drawing unwanted attention from regulatory agencies and endangering the relationship.

The deal with R.J. Reynolds was indeed a touchdown—or checkered flag—for both partners. RJR had a growing sport to tie its name to and use as a marketing vehicle. The cigarette manufacturer would have the opportunity to reach larger and larger TV audiences, and, when the Motorsports Racing Network (MRN) was inaugurated in 1971, radio audiences as well. Sales of Winston cigarettes rose, along with an unprecedented degree of fan-to-brand loyalty. For NASCAR, this was the infusion the series had needed to keep going and growing. The alliance with Reynolds, although drastically different from the factory deals, positioned NASCAR with a serious corporate partner once more—one that would positively develop NASCAR's potential. The credibility that RJR brought to the series would eventually attract other companies. After all, if a corporation as large and prosperous as R.J. Reynolds was on the NASCAR bandwagon...

Perhaps most important, the new partnership brought stability to the sport. France's vision for NASCAR fit well with RJR's goals in sponsoring it, so the two were able to work cooperatively toward those goals. Another feature of the relationship that stands out in hindsight is its longevity: twenty-seven of NASCAR's fifty years have been in partnership with RJR and Winston. A relationship spanning that many years allows long-range planning and the careful, measured execution of goals. With this spirit of teamwork, R.J. Reynolds launched NASCAR into what is known as its "modern era."

Still Some Rough Patches Despite the boost in the overall health of NASCAR racing that resulted from RJR's involvement, 1971 was a year of uncertainty for many racing teams and tracks. Teams that had prospered as factory representatives were used to receiving parts and assistance from the auto companies up front. That would no longer be the case. Though RJR would sink more money into NASCAR, it would be a longer-term investment, and not targeted as directly to the race teams. The improved purses would come only after the races had been run, and the $100,000 Winston Cup points fund would be awarded only three times a year—$25,000 in May, $25,000 in September, and the remainder at the end of the season. Very few teams had enough cash in hand to make it to the big paydays; for many, the only source of funding other than their own wallets was the appearance money paid to drivers at some events.

So teams that either still had factory sponsorship (by 1971, that meant Richard Petty) or were able to acquire other corporate sponsorship were at a significant advantage. In the face of that situation, many drivers and teams looked seriously at closing their shops: Banjo Matthews and the famous Holman-Moody operation were among those who closed their doors before the next season began. Premier driver Cale Yarborough jumped ship to race Indy cars, feeling that no quality rides were available in NASCAR. This dramatic disparity between teams was borne out by Petty's dominance of the 1971 season—he left everyone else running for second, as he won twenty-one events and handily captured the first Winston Cup championship.

The Winston Cup Series

To make sure it got the most bang for its buck, Reynolds decided to sponsor only a subset of the GN series. At the time there were forty-eight races in the Grand National season, many of which were still short races run on dirt tracks. While all races in the schedule counted toward the points standings and the points fund, Winston would only directly sponsor

Page 22: Bobby Isaac had great success driving for Nord Krauskopf's #71 team, winning thirty-six races between 1967 and 1972. Here, he emerges from the car after qualifying on the pole for the May 1972 Talladega race. Think those shoes were fireproof? PAGE 23: *Roger Penske has long been a driving force in American racing. In 1972 he added the Winston Cup schedule to his competitive calendar. As both team owner and track owner, he has helped influence the growth of the Winston Cup over the last three decades.* ABOVE: *NASCAR has entertained a number of government luminaries over the years. Here, Secretary of Defense Melvin Laird looks over Charlie Glotzbach's #3 car with Bill France before the start of the 1969 Firecracker 400 at Daytona.*

or promote races of 250 miles (400km) or more. This subset was called the Winston Cup series.

Clearly, the days were numbered for many of the small tracks that had been part of NASCAR's history since its inception. The small tracks and short races couldn't provide the type of exposure Reynolds was looking for, nor could they survive very long on their own outside the Winston Cup series. By 1972, the full Winston Grand National series was cut back from forty-eight to thirty-one races, all of them run on asphalt and all 250 miles (400km) or longer. Greenville-Pickens, Bowman-Gray, and other tracks that had been run since the 1950s were cut from the schedule entirely. The only remaining short tracks were Martinsville, Richmond, Bristol, and North Wilkesboro. Fortunately, NASCAR realized that short-track racing is a vital part of stock car tradition and beloved by fans. Aside from North Wilkesboro, which closed at the end of the 1996 season, the other short tracks have prospered and each still hosts two races in the Winston Cup series today.

An interesting wrinkle in the NASCAR/RJR relationship was that, even though both organizations came from the same geographic area and shared their customer base to a large degree, in the beginning, southern sports writers resisted referring to the series as the Winston Grand National or the Winston Cup, whether out of respect for tradition or disdain for the tobacco tie-in. Over time that has changed, as the relationship has solidified, and new generations of fans have come to the sport knowing it only as the Winston Cup. Today "The Winston Cup" stands for NASCAR racing, and any association with a brand of cigarettes is only in the back of most race fans' minds, if it is there at all.

A Change in Leadership

At the start of the 1972 season, NASCAR was heading into its twenty-fourth year as a sanctioning body. One of the advantages the organization had enjoyed was uniformity of purpose and vision in its leadership. The reason for this was very simple—"Big Bill" France had been the only hand at the helm since NASCAR's formation.

By 1972, France was ready to pass the baton. On January 11, at sixty-two years of age, France retired as president of NASCAR. Luckily for the organization, the handoff was smooth. William Clifton France, known by most as "Bill Jr.," would be the new top man. Bill Jr. had grown up with NASCAR and had been involved in all facets of its administration. Equally important, he shared his father's vision for its future: "I am sure NASCAR will not only grow but accelerate in its leadership in the sport of automobile racing," he said in his inaugural address.

Nor would the elder France be gone entirely from the scene. Bill Sr. would stay on as an advisor and as president of the company that ran the Daytona and Talladega speedways—International Speedway Corporation.

Benny Parsons (whose #72 Chevy passes Jimmy Crawford's #22) left the October 1973 "National 500" at Charlotte with a 194-point championship lead. He finished a respectable fourth in the race, though he was four laps down to the winner, Cale Yarborough.

Fine-Tuning the Series

Though NASCAR had a firm sense of direction with its new sponsor and an energetic new leader to carry its agenda, the sport still had rough spots to smooth out.

In 1972, all events less than 250 miles (402.3km) long were removed from the Winston GN series schedule. The reduction in the number of Winston Grand National races was actually a relief for most teams, since the expense of running several races in the same week had become prohibitive. With the new schedule they ran only one race a week, and the series ended in November instead of December. The Daytona Twin 125 qualifying races remained in the series, but were no longer considered points races.

NASCAR's attempts to rework the points system turned into an annual event itself, as NASCAR tried different schemes, each designed to achieve a particular goal—whether rewarding drivers for running to win, participating in many races, or racing consistently.

As NASCAR looked at the points standings at the end of each year and compared them to "what really happened," it repeatedly found that it needed to adjust the calculation method. In 1974, Bob Latford, a public relations employee at Atlanta and other NASCAR tracks, came up with a fair and practical plan—one that would make sense to drivers and fans alike. His method, first used in the 1975 season, reflected the changes in the NASCAR schedule. For the first time, all events would award an equal number of points.

The scheme favors drivers who consistently race hard and finish near the front; it is no longer enough just to start (in 1970 and 1971, there was a rash of teams running just a few laps to collect points, then pulling out of the race). The scheme remains in place today, unchanged since 1975. Although drivers and fans periodically lobby for bonus points for the race winner, most teams are satisfied that their points standings fairly represent their performance through the season.

Leveling the Playing Field

NASCAR's administration of the rules relative to the different manufacturers—whether it was Dodge versus Chevy in 1972 or Monte Carlo versus Taurus in 1998—has been less than universally accepted over the years. Most of the time the dissatisfaction is just an undercurrent, but the rules tend to come under fire in times of financial stress, when teams are more acutely aware of the money they're missing by not running as well as they feel they could be. That was exactly the situation in the early 1970s.

As they say, you can't please all of the people all of the time. Big Bill France found that to be very much the case when he tried to balance the demands of the auto manufacturers in the 1960s. Bill Jr. learned the same lesson during his attempts to level the playing field for race teams in the first half of the 1970s.

NASCAR began adjusting the rules on engines and carburetor restrictor plates in 1972, to try to compensate for the differences between makes of cars. The rules and procedures were tested sharply in 1973, when NASCAR mandated new carburetor sleeves to offset the advantage of the Chrysler Hemi engines. Recall that Richard Petty and Buddy Baker (in a Petty-owned car) were the only teams still enjoying factory sponsorship at the time. The independents—that is, everyone else—were struggling to make ends meet against what was perceived to be the unfair advantage of Petty's "exotic racing engines." The changes helped equalize the field somewhat, allowing Chevy to find success for the first time since Junior Johnson's Mystery Motor made a splash in 1963. The changes also heightened the tension among teams, because it was pretty obvious that quite a bit of rule-bending was going on as teams on shoestring budgets looked for any way to get an advantage and bolster their winnings.

The situation finally came to a head at Charlotte. Pole-sitter Charlie Glotzbach had to requalify when an illegal carburetor plate was found in his car. Then NASCAR withheld the results of a postrace inspection of winner Cale Yarborough's Richard Howard/Junior Johnson #11 Chevy, Petty's #43 Dodge, and Bobby Allison's #12 Chevy for several days. There was finally an announcement that at least one of the cars (unofficially, #11) was illegal, but since it had passed the prerace inspection the results would stand.

The resulting uproar forced NASCAR to re-evaluate and tighten prerace and postrace inspection procedures, as well as the process for dealing with infringements. Even so, it took a long "come to Jesus meeting" with Bill France to convince Bobby Allison not to boycott the rest of the season.

Winston Cup Championship Money

R.J. Reynolds has repeatedly demonstrated its commitment to NASCAR's Winston Cup with its financial backing. In 1971, Winston established a $100,000 points fund for the top twenty drivers in the standings, an awesome figure considering that the 1970 champion, Bobby Isaac, earned less than $200,000 in the entire season. Since then, the Winston Cup points fund has increased dramatically. Reynolds has also provided other funding specifically to help teams, such as the Winner's Circle plan, and sponsored special events like the Winston Select race and the annual awards banquet at the Waldorf-Astoria Hotel in New York.

Here's how the numbers have gone:

1971–1972: $100,000 in three parts ($25,000 in May and $25,000 in September to the top ten in points, and $50,000 to the top twenty at year's end)

1973–1974: $120,000 (Benny Parsons collected $40,000 as the 1973 champion)

1975–1977: $150,000 (RJR also started the Winner's Circle plan this year, paying selected teams $3,000 to appear at superspeedway events and $2,000 for short tracks. Other teams in the top twenty got $500 or $250 to appear. The catch was that you had to plan to race the entire schedule. In 1976, the plan was changed so that any team winning a race in the previous year qualified for the larger amounts)

1978–1979: $175,000

1980–1981: $210,000 (Winner's Circle fund up to $3,900 and $3,200)

1982: $300,000

1983–1984: $500,000 (1983 champion Bobby Allison collected $150,000)

1985: $750,000 ($250,000 to Darrell Waltrip on top of the points. This was the season that put Winston Cup racing on the front of most magazines in America. RJR offered a $1,000,000 bonus to any driver who could, in the same year, win three out of four "prestige" events—the Daytona 500 [the most famous race], the World 600 [the longest race], the Talladega 500 [the fastest race], and the Southern 500 [the oldest race]. A consolation prize of $100,000 was instituted, to be awarded to any driver winning two of the four.

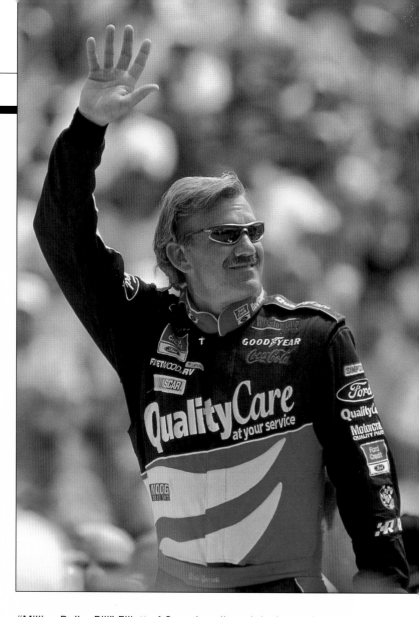

"Million Dollar Bill" Elliott of Georgia collected the bonus in its first year. Although several drivers would collect the consolation award, the Winston Million would remain secure for twelve more years.)

1986–1988: $2,000,000

1989–1992: $2,500,000 (Rusty Wallace earned an even $1,000,000 for the champion share in 1989)

1993–1994: $3,000,000

1995: $3,500,000

1996–1997: $4,000,000 (in 1997 Jeff Gordon became the second winner of the Winston Million)

1998: $5,000,000 (RJR added the Indianapolis race to the list and restructured the Winston Million to be the "No Bull 5": any of the top five finishers in the previous qualifying race could collect $1,000,000 by winning the next. Thus, up to $5,000,000 a year could be awarded. In addition, each time a driver wins, a fan is selected to receive $1,000,000 as well. The new fund was hit hard in its first year—Jeff Gordon won twice and Dale Jarrett won once. In the course of winninng his third championship, Jeff Gordon picked up $2,000,000 from the points fund alone, winning $6,000,000 overall.)

The following year, 1974, was a roller coaster ride of rule changes as NASCAR tried to address the issues. The administration didn't issue any changes before the season, as it worked through the OPEC oil embargo, but by the end of the year NASCAR published five changes to the rules governing racing engines.

The new rules focused on the disparity between big engines (366 cubic inches or more) and small engines. The first change replaced the restrictor plate with a smaller carburetor for the big engines. The reaction was predictable—teams running smaller engines lauded the move, while Petty and others running the big engines decried it. NASCAR readjusted, giving the large engines a bit more carb. There was some improvement, but still not parity. The next change specified two different carburetors for the big engines, based on the size of the track. Midway through the season, NASCAR announced that the maximum size for smaller engines would be 358 cubic inches.

By this time everyone was confused and frustrated by the frequent changes. "They ought to make rules and stick by them," was Junior Johnson's reaction. The biggest impact was on the independent teams, who had to go through expensive retooling each time a new set of rules was announced.

What NASCAR really wanted to do was get rid of the big engines—remnants of the out-of-control developments of the 1960s—altogether. By year's end, the maximum size for any engine in the series was 358 cubic inches.

The Oil Embargo

There had been no auto racing in the United States during World War II, because oil and gasoline were precious commodities and in limited supply; racing, deemed an extravagant use of resources necessary to the war effort, was stopped. The year 1974 threatened to echo that situation, albeit to a far lesser degree. In the fall of 1973, the Organization of the Petroleum Exporting Countries (OPEC) had announced an embargo on oil exports to the United States, Europe, Japan, and other nations that had supported Israel in the recent war in the Middle East. Henceforth, OPEC announced, it would no longer negotiate price increases with oil companies, but would set prices unilaterally.

OPPOSITE: *Dale Jarrett was the last Winston Cup champion of the twentieth century.* BELOW: *Among Indy car racers who made the transition to NASCAR, A.J. Foyt did it the most often and was the most successful, with seven wins in 128 starts. Here, he waits to qualify for the March 1972 race at California's Ontario Motor Speedway, where he set a new qualifying record and won the race.*

When the U.S. government began regulating the sale of gasoline, France and officers from other motorsports organizations decided to take proactive steps. NASCAR, USAC, NHRA (National Hot Rod Association), SCCA (Sports Car Club of America), and IMSA (International Motor Sports Association) formed the National Motorsports Committee, and representatives gathered to come up with a way to keep the cars on track.

At the time, the government didn't have much hard data on the consumption of gasoline by different activities, and in the absence of information, many people assumed that auto racing topped the gas-guzzler list. To counter this negative perception, the National Motorsports Committee prepared a report showing the estimated gas consumption by a number of leisure and sporting activities.

The list was an eye-opener. In first place was vacation travel, which consumed more than 5 billion gallons (18.9 billion l) annually. Auto racing, in seventh place with about 93 million gallons (352 million l) a year, trailed behind football, baseball, horse racing, theater attendance, and nonscheduled aviation. The Federal Energy Commission was grateful for the information and commended the auto racing community for "their foresight in compiling figures on energy consumption in sports and leisure time areas."

The next step was to set standards for voluntary reductions in fuel usage by the racing groups. Realizing that racing was still in a vulnerable position and that there was only a limited window of time during which they could set their own guidelines before the government stepped in, the group moved quickly to come up with a proposal. The result was a commitment to reduce gasoline use in motorsports by 25 percent. Race distances would be cut by 10 percent, prerace practice and testing sessions would be reduced, and some special events, such as the 24 Hours of Daytona race, would be cancelled.

The embargo certainly had an effect on NASCAR, as it did on most aspects of life, for the next few years. Attendance at races decreased at the beginning of the season, but not disastrously so, and was likely due as much to the new restrictions on gas sales—pumps were closed on Sundays—as to changes in race activities. Even so, the setback was only temporary. By July, NASCAR announced that it had already met its projected fuel savings for the year, and the remaining races would be run at full length.

Donnie Allison was one of the many top drivers to pilot Bud Moore's cars over the years. Allison joined the #15 team for six races in 1972 but only scored one top ten finish. Moore's blue and white Fords wouldn't make it to victory lane until 1975, with Buddy Baker at the wheel.

1971: Petty Runs Away from the Field and Wins His Third Championship

With Chrysler's backing, Richard Petty was an unstoppable force in 1971, although at the start of the season it had looked as if NASCAR's tinkering with the rules might have resulted in some level of parity between Ford and Chrysler. The year began with a surprise win at Riverside by West Coast driver Ray Elders (the first of his two career wins) followed by a pair of Plymouth wins (Petty and Pete Hamilton) and a pair by Mercury (Pearson and Foyt).

Those races had apparently been mere warm-ups for Petty and his powder blue #43. Despite further adjustments to the restrictor plate rules, Petty went on to nail twenty more wins, including a string of five in a row through July and August. The other Petty car—Buddy Baker's #11 Dodge—picked up one of the few remaining victories.

After the March Rebel 400 at Darlington, David Pearson walked out of his Holman-Moody ride. Looking to cut expenses so they could get along without Ford backing, Holman-Moody had trimmed back its schedule and Pearson's percentage of up-front appearance money. Pearson, who had managed only two wins that year, went with what looked like a good deal with Chris Vallo to drive Pontiacs for the rest of the year. The team never really got it together, however, so the "Silver Fox" was in search of yet another ride for the next year.

With Pearson effectively sidelined, Petty's closest competition came from Bobby Allison. When the Holman-Moody ride opened up, Allison, who had been running his own Dodges that year, went for it. The combination

---

OPPOSITE: *At the start of the 1971 season Bobby Allison was running his own Dodge team with premium sponsorship from Coca-Cola, one of the few big ticket sponsors at the time. He was winless going into May of that year, though, so he jumped to the open Holman-Moody Ford team, taking his sponsor with him.* BELOW: *The #12 team's win in the 1971 Talladega 500 was their eighth of eleven that year. Here the crew hitches a ride to victory lane.*

clicked, and Allison promptly ripped off a string of five consecutive wins of his own. The two spent the last half of the year banging fenders as they found themselves competing for the lead week after week. By season's end, Allison's eleven wins were enough to pull him up to fourth in the points standing.

The impact of the newly established Winston Cup series was felt almost immediately. None of the top drivers competed in all forty-eight races in the 1971 GN schedule. Frank Warren ran the most—forty-seven. Petty and Cecil Gordon each ran forty-six, and most drivers ran far fewer. But despite having run fewer races, Petty dominated the season, winning his third Grand National and the very first Winston Cup championship by a good margin over James Hylton.

1971 Championship Standings

Place	Car#	Driver	Car Type	Points
1	43	Richard Petty	Plymouth	4,435
2	48	James Hylton	Ford	4,071
3	24	Cecil Gordon	Mercury	3,677
4	12	Bobby Allison	Ford	3,636
5	64	Elmo Langley	Mercury	3,356
6	25	Jabe Thomas	Plymouth	3,200
7	10	Bill Champion	Ford	3,058
8	79	Frank Warren	Dodge	2,886
9	70	J.D. McDuffie	Chevy	2,862
10	30	Walter Ballard	Ford	2,633

Richard Petty and the #43

So much has been said and written about "King" Richard Petty, son of stock car pioneer and three-time champion Lee Petty, that it's hard to add to the official record. Seven-time champion and seven-time Daytona 500 winner, with two hundred career wins overall—the amazing statistics still don't come near to portraying the man. Petty may well be the best spokesman and representative a sport has ever had. It's a fitting tribute, for instance, that the statue at Atlanta dedicated to him depicts him not hunkered down in a race car but signing an autograph for a young girl. It's been estimated that Petty has signed his name for fans more than any other human being in history. Years after his retirement, he's still one of the most popular figures among NASCAR fans, and the drivers of the #43 STP Pontiac have found themselves crowd favorites merely for being in his car.

Petty's introduction to the Grand National circuit came in 1958, when he drove the #142. He first drove the famous #43 in 1959 and scored the first win of his thirty-five-year driving career the next year. Petty's achievements began well before the modern era: he won championships in 1964, 1967, and 1971, and had an unparalleled twenty-seven victories in 1967 in his blue Plymouth Belvedere. With the modern era came Petty's first Winston Cup championship, in 1972 (its first year); ultimately, he would win three more times.

Some of the sport's greatest moments, events that have defined NASCAR's history, have featured Richard Petty—for example, the wild finish of the 1976 Daytona 500, where Petty and David Pearson awed TV viewers nationwide when they crashed during the last lap. Then there was Petty's 200th win at Daytona, with President Ronald Reagan cheering him on.

Although Petty retired as a driver in 1992, he continues to field red and blue #43 STP machines as team owner. One last note: the famous "Petty blue" originated in 1959, when Petty, wanting to paint his car something other than white, found he didn't have enough blue paint to cover the vehicle. So he stretched the blue by adding white, ending up with his signature color.

OPPOSITE: *Over his thirty-five-year career, Richard Petty has driven just about every make of stock car: Plymouth, Dodge, Ford, Chevy, Oldsmobile, Buick, and Pontiac. Petty's best season came in 1967 in this Plymouth Belvedere. The car, which won twenty-seven races that year, was actually a 1966 Belvedere with 1967-vintage sheet metal over it.* ABOVE: *One of Petty's favorite cars was the sleek Dodge Charger that he drove between 1972 and 1977. Petty piloted the Charger, with new sponsorship from STP and a new red and blue paint scheme, to three championships and forty-five wins. The 1976 Daytona 500, shown here, was one of the few races that got away from him that year.* LEFT: *Petty spent the last ten years of his career in Pontiacs. The STP team switched to GM after the Magnum, and switched from Buick to Pontiac in 1982. They had struggled with Buicks, and Pontiac offered better support to the team. The 1992 Grand Prix shown here was the car that the King drove in his last season as a driver.*

1972: Petty Starts the Modern Era with Another Championship

Although R.J. Reynolds and Winston first became involved with NASCAR in 1971, the start of the "modern era" of stock car racing is usually counted as 1972. That was the year that NASCAR abandoned the dirt tracks and 100-mile (160km) races, and the schedule was reduced to just the thirty-one Winston Cup events. Because the number of races each year since then has remained in that ballpark, NASCAR records are most often counted from then forward.

There were quite a few rule changes in 1972, too, and whether because of them or in spite of them, the competition was actually tighter than it had been in the previous year.

The 1972 season started without one of the longest-standing and best-respected teams in the NASCAR garages. The Ford factory pullout in 1970 finally caught up with the Holman-Moody team, which had been building winning Fords since the fifties, and they closed their doors before the 1972 season opener. Bobby Allison found himself without a ride, but with the Coca-Cola sponsorship. The Richard Howard/Junior Johnson team had a driver—Charlie Glotzbach—but needed money. Glotzbach found himself on the outside, and Johnson started turning the wrenches on the red and gold #12 Chevys for Allison.

Petty started off the year much as he had finished the previous one—by winning. He snagged the shortened opener at Riverside, red-flagged for poor visibility due to fog on the track. In all, he earned eight wins and his fourth championship that year, but with Allison and Pearson hooked up with solid teams, he found the competition much tougher than it had been the previous year.

When Chrysler's backing faded for Petty, he found a new corporate sponsor to keep his team competitive. Petty and STP began the longest team-sponsor relationship in NASCAR's history that year, but there were some tough points to negotiate in the deal. Andy Granatelli wanted the cars painted STP red, while Petty insisted on retaining the familiar Petty blue. The two compromised, and for the next twenty-six years #43 would sport different combinations of blue and red.

A.J. Foyt started the year off once again with the Wood Brothers. He had replaced Donnie Allison in that ride for several races in 1971, winning two events. The team continued running well in 1972, winning the Daytona 500, then weeks later the Miller High Life 500, at Ontario, California, for the second straight year. Foyt led all but thirty-three laps in the Daytona race and was the only one on the lead lap at the finish. Despite the team's success,

however, Foyt's heart was with Indy car racing, and he left the premier ride right after the Ontario win to concentrate on USAC racing. Foyt would toy with NASCAR racing over the next decade and a half, running his own cars occasionally, but he never again enjoyed a victory.

With the Wood Brothers ride open, David Pearson lost no time making himself available. After leaving the struggling Holman-Moody shop in 1971, he had a dismal second half of that season in Chris Vallo's underpowered Pontiacs. He started 1972 without a regular ride on the circuit, but when he joined the #21 team in April 1972, one of the most successful driver-team combinations in NASCAR's modern era was formed. Throughout the duration of the partnership, between 1972 and 1979, the maroon and white Purolator-sponsored Mercurys would pick up forty-three wins and fifty-one poles, a stunning 30 percent win ratio and 36 percent pole ratio. The year 1972 was typical of that average, with Pearson gathering six wins in just fourteen starts in the car, including his very first ride with them, at the Darlington Rebel 500 in April.

The season had settled into a pattern, with the wins being taken in round robin fashion by Petty, Pearson, and

Bobby Allison spent the 1972 season running for Richard Howard and Junior Johnson. This winner's circle celebration for the Nashville 420, one of ten that season, was a family affair—Allison's sons Davey (on the right) and Clifford (left) look on. Davey would put that day's observations of victory lane protocol to good use, celebrating eighteen wins of his own.

Allison (with Bobby Isaac's last win, at Rockingham, and Ray Elder's second, and last, win thrown in). The races at Talladega provided some points of interest, as they often do. The first race, in May, featured one of the strangest instances of alleged cheating ever to occur in NASCAR history, not least because the driver made the accusations against himself. Marty Robbins, a successful country singer and Winston Cup rookie, qualified for the race at 174 mph (280kph). When he found himself passing cars during the race at about 188 mph (303kph), he thought something might be wrong. Robbins finished eighteenth and was awarded rookie-of-the-race awards, but was concerned that he might have achieved those wins illegally—unintentionally, but still illegally.

Robbins asked Bill Gazaway, the NASCAR technical inspector, to tear down his engine after the race, and Robbins was eventually disqualified. Practically defining good sportsmanship, Robbins not only didn't gripe about the outcome (an error in setting up the engine had given him a boost), but also talked about the kick he had gotten out of learning how fast he could drive a car. The May race was also noteworthy for its thirty-eighth-place

Darrell Waltrip broke into the Winston Cup ranks in 1972. He brought a 1969 Mercury that he bought for $12,500 from the Holman & Moody shop. Waltrip has wrecked the car in an ARCA race at Talladega and rebuilt it as a 1971 to make it eligible for the cup race. The car had a number of H&M "special touches" that made it hard to use stock parts for the repairs.

1972 Championship Standings

Place	Car#	Driver	Car Type	Points
1	43	Richard Petty	Plymouth	8701.40
2	12	Bobby Allison	Chevy	8573.50
3	48	James Hylton	Ford	8158.70
4	24	Cecil Gordon	Mercury	7326.05
5	72	Benny Parsons	Mercury	6844.15
6	30	Walter Ballard	Ford	6781.45
7	64	Elmo Langley	Ford	6656.25
8	4	John Sears	Plymouth	6298.50
9	7	Dean Dalton	Mercury	6295.05
10	76	Ben Arnold	Ford	6179.00

David Pearson

They say no one ever remembers who came in second, but in David Pearson's case, being second on the all-time NASCAR win list after Richard Petty has certainly not relegated him to obscurity.

Pearson had a patient, canny driving style. The "Silver Fox" would often lay back and save his equipment until just the right moment in a race, then seemingly come out of nowhere to capture the win. His style best suited the super-speedway races of the late sixties and seventies, when he garnered an astounding sixty-four poles and fifty-one wins.

He broke into the big leagues in 1961, winning the World 600 and then the Firecracker 400 a month later in Ray Fox's Pontiacs. From 1962 through 1966, Pearson drove Cotton Owens' prepped #6 Dodges, and after sitting out 1965 with the Chrysler NASCAR boycott, he roared back in 1966 to win sixteen races and his first GN championship.

In 1967, Pearson replaced Fred Lorenzen in the Holman-Moody #17 Fords then went on to win two more championships, in 1968 and 1969. When Ford pulled out of racing in 1970, and the Holman-Moody shop starting cutting back, Pearson moved on. Partway through the 1972 season Pearson hooked up with the Wood Brothers and started another successful chapter in his career. Although the #21 Mercury team never ran enough of the Winston Cup schedule to seriously contend for the championship, the team took forty-three trophies by winning nearly every event it entered.

Following a communication breakdown during a race, Pearson broke up with the team in 1979, and thereafter fielded his own cars, with Chattanooga Chew sponsorship on and off through 1986. Pearson officially retired in 1989.

ABOVE: *After leaving the Wood Brothers in 1979, Pearson ran short seasons for Rod Osterlund and Hoss Ellington. He hooked up with Joel Halpern in 1981. He is shown here in 1981 comparing notes with legendary mechanic Jake Elders.*
LEFT: *Throughout his twenty-seven-year Grand National and Winston Cup career, David Pearson (center) rarely ran a full schedule of races. Had he done so he could well have equaled Petty's performance in wins and championships.*

The Winston Cup's first Rookie of the Year, Larry Smith, was killed in a seemingly minor crash in the 1973 Talladega 500. Smith's #92 Mercury was sponsored by Carling Brewery. Here he poses with the Carling Darling for a publicity shot.

finisher, a young fellow out of Tennessee running his first Winston Cup event: Darrell Waltrip.

The August Talladega race was highlighted by underdog James Hylton's win. Hylton had had one previous win, in 1970, and although he placed well in the points through the first half of the 1970s, it was more by running top-tens than by racing for the lead. Of his Talladega victory, Hylton observed: "I hope people will realize that I race as hard as I can. I proved that today."

As the season moved into the short-track segment in the autumn, it became increasingly clear that Petty and Allison had a feud going. At Richmond, then Martinsville, then North Wilkesboro, the two repeatedly ran together, leading the pack by several laps. With no one else to worry about, they wrangled the wins between themselves. Petty managed to win all three events, but only by outlasting Allison in their ongoing bumper duels. After the North Wilkesboro slugfest, neither racer bothered denying that there was a feud between them, but they attributed it to the close quarters of short-track racing. It was expected that the rivalry would cool off a little when they moved on to Charlotte.

The excitement generated by Allison and Petty distracted public attention from a remarkable fact about their stats. As of the thirtieth race of the year, at Rockingham, Bobby Allison had led in thirty-nine consecutive events. Although Allison outgunned Petty in the wins department, ten to eight, and in laps led, Petty finished more miles, which, according to that year's points system, gave him the edge for the championship.

1973: A Surprise Champion in a Year of Turmoil

The 1973 season was characterized by upset. Only twenty-eight races were run, with Texas World Speedway reduced to one event and the races in Ontario and Trenton canceled. Trenton was never rescheduled after being rained out on its original date. Changes in the rules played an even larger role in 1973 than in 1972, and excited more controversy. And added to all of that, there was a tremendous amount of ride-swapping and coming and going among drivers.

The most interesting event of the year, though, was the race for the championship. Benny Parsons, who had only been driving on the circuit full-time since 1970, and up to then with only moderate success, now found himself in contention for the championship. In the spring, Parsons began repeatedly racking up top-fives and top-tens. Over the course of the season, he won only one race; in fact, the only time he finished on the lead lap of a race was during that win. The points system in place that year rewarded consistency, however, so Parsons' twenty-one top-tens were enough for him to hold his lead.

The number of driver-team changes in 1973 made it a classic "silly season." Bobby Isaac had left the Nord Krauskopf #71 K&K Insurance team after the 1972 season to drive Bud Moore's #15 Fords. Krauskopf had pulled out and come back several times during rules squabbles. That—and K&K's plans to run a two-car team in 1973 (which didn't materialize)—had prompted Isaac's departure.

Buddy Baker took over the #71 ride. STP was sponsoring only the #43, and Chrysler wasn't there to back Baker's #11, so the second team was dissolved, and Baker (dubbed the "Gentle Giant" despite his mercurial temper) had moved on. Petty wouldn't run a second team again until his son, Kyle, came on the scene, in 1979.

Despite their many successes together, Bobby Allison had departed the Junior Johnson team at the end of 1972, electing to form his own team, still #12, with Coca-Cola as sponsor. Reputedly, Johnson and Allison had had a quirky, if successful, relationship. Allison once commented that Johnson never spoke directly to him, even in his presence, but would always talk to him through someone else. Whether this was the reason for the split, or whether it came about because Allison felt more comfortable guiding his own destiny, he left Johnson looking for a new driver for 1973. It wouldn't be the last time that Allison ran his own team.

Luckily, Johnson didn't have to look far. In a surprise move, Cale Yarborough rejoined NASCAR and took the new #11 ride (with Kar-Kare as sponsor) with Johnson. Yarborough had left NASCAR at the end of 1970 to race in USAC. After 1972, his team owner, Gene White, decided to reduce his stable from two cars to one, and Cale was the odd man out. He returned to his roots, and was immediately successful with the new partnership.

Jabe Thomas and Benny Parsons duel on a superspeedway in 1973. Thomas drove the #25 Dodge for Don Robertson; Parsons was in the L.G. DeWitt #72 car. Parsons' team pulled off one of the most unlikely championships of the series' history that year.

The start of the season, at Riverside, witnessed the arrival on the scene of an important new team owned by a newcomer to NASCAR. In 1972, Roger Penske, deciding to give stock car racing a try, fielded rides for Donnie Allison, Dave Marcis, and Mark Donohue. We're not talking your typical Chevys, Fords, or Plymouths, though—Penske's red, white, and blue #16s were AMC Matadors. The pundits in the garage initially scoffed at the notion of an AMC entry, but the team scored a win in what was only Donohue's fifth outing, and when Penske later hooked up with highly respected drivers like Bobby Allison, the Matador acquired a fan following of its own.

Once again, familiar names—Petty, Pearson, and Yarborough—were capturing the wins week after week. Bobby Allison enjoyed less success, however, winning only two races that year. The Wood Brothers, luckily for everyone else, ran only a limited schedule of eighteen events, winning an eye-popping eleven of those eighteen. The

Wood Brothers car was so dominant that Pearson took the April Rebel 500 at Darlington by thirteen laps over second-place Benny Parsons. Yarborough and Johnson had intermittent success in their first year, taking four wins but not snagging enough top spots to secure the points lead. Petty had, for him, an off-year, winning only six races and finishing well down in the points (fifth, the lowest he'd finished since 1961, except for 1965, when he had boycotted NASCAR).

Parsons got his second career win at Bristol, and then the season took an odd twist once more when the teams hit Talladega. Relative unknown Dick Brooks collected his first win in the August race. Brooks was filling in for driver-owner Jim Crawford (at NASCAR's request) and, despite going down a lap twice during the race, was able to take the lead with fewer than ten laps to go and hold on for the win. Unfortunately, the race also had a tragic side. What looked like a routine crash on lap 9, involving 1972's Rookie of the Year, Larry Smith, turned out to be much more serious: Smith suffered fatal injuries in the impact.

Later in the same race, Bobby Isaac decided it was time to hang up his helmet—not after the race, but during it. On lap 90, Isaac radioed owner Bud Moore, "Get a relief driver. I quit." Isaac parked the car in the pits, climbed out, and told Moore he was quitting racing; he later commented, "Something told me to quit. I don't know anything else to do but abide by it." When questioned about his action, Isaac, the 1970 GN champion, retorted, "I don't have anything to prove to myself or anyone else. I know how it feels to want to drive and I know how it feels to win and lose. I know how it feels to be a champion and now I know how it feels to quit." Isaac would return for a handful of races with Banjo Matthews between 1974 and 1976, but didn't seriously compete. He retired completely, with thirty-seven career wins, after the Charlotte race in May 1976. Darrell Waltrip was given the chance to finish the year in Moore's #15 car.

Though Parsons had a decent lead going into the home stretch at Rockingham, the championship was up for grabs until nearly the end of the race. Early on, Parsons, caught up in someone else's wreck, lost the entire right side of his car—including the rollcage. Despite the apparent impossibility of holding on to their points lead, the team set to work repairing the car, which had already logged 136 laps. Eventually, the car was in decent enough shape to safely roll around the track, accumulating laps and points. Richard Petty, who was second in points coming into the race, also had trouble, which dropped him from second to fifth in the standings. The amazing effort from his crew was enough to earn Parsons the championship by sixty-seven points.

Roger Penske backed AMC Matadors for several drivers between 1972 and 1975. Mark Donohue gave the Matador its first win at the beginning of 1973 at Riverside, California. Dave Marcis took over the seat later that year and the number was changed from #16 to #2.

Figuring the Points

One of Bill France's fundamental goals when he founded NASCAR was to establish a unified championship ranking of drivers. All sanctioned races would award points according to a published standard that would accumulate from race to race, with the series champion being the driver who had the most points at the end of the season. Every driver, owner, and fan should be able to tell how a team's performance from week to week affected its position in the standings. A high points standing was important to the teams, not only for the prestige and bragging rights it conferred, but because points fund moneys increased as a team rose to the top. And, of course, the champions and runners-up would be the ones who attracted the top-dollar sponsors or factory backers.

This all seems pretty straightforward. But the key word with NASCAR has always been "competitiveness," and the points system has often been used to keep the level of competition high. To that end, NASCAR has manipulated the points structure in different ways in order to guide the behavior of teams as they strive to meet certain goals in competition. As a result, the way points have been awarded over the years has changed as NASCAR has faced different challenges and tried different approaches to keeping the racing tight. In some cases, for instance, the points system rewarded drivers for entering the most or even all races, while at other times, racing flat-out for the win was what yielded the most points.

While it sounds obvious, there's no doubt that the rivalries of the 1970s were heavily affected by the way the points were figured. Because today's points system has been in place for more than twenty years, it's hard to appreciate how drivers felt when the points system changed—and changed drastically—each year through the first half of the 1970s. And because of this constantly shifting landscape, it wasn't always immediately evident to drivers and teams what they needed to do to win the most points.

Let's take a look at how the points have been calculated through the modern era. Note that the system is geared for drivers, not teams or owners, so even if a driver has raced with more than one team in a season, whatever points they earn from race to race count toward their year-end total.

1971: At the start of the Winston GN and Winston Cup, points were awarded based on finishing position in each race. The number of points awarded for a given position depended on the length of the race, though, so drivers winning the big race had a distinct advantage.

For race lengths of
- More than 400 miles (644km): 150 points for 1st place, with each position earning 3 points less than the previous one (147, 144, 141, etc.)
- 250–399 miles (402–643km): 100 points for 1st, dropping by 2 points per position
- 100–249 miles (161–401km): 50 points for 1st, dropping by 1 point per position

1972: To keep drivers running for entire races (there had been a number of "parkouts" in 1970 and 1971, that is, drivers pulled out of races after running only long enough to get decent points), the points scheme was changed drastically. Points would now be calculated based on the number of laps run in a race and the length of the track.

Length of track	Points awarded per lap
• less than 1 mile (1.6km)	0.25
• 1 mile (1.6km)	0.5
• 1.3 miles (2.1km)	0.7
• 1.5 miles (2.4km)	0.75
• 2 miles (3.2km)	1
• 2.5 miles (4km) and up	1.25

1973: The same scheme used in 1972 but with a 25-point bonus for winning the race.

1974: When Benny Parsons captured the 1973 championship after winning only one race, and finishing in the lead lap only in that win, NASCAR decided another change was called for. The new points scheme was the most convoluted yet. The formula was as follows:

- (Total prize money earned year-to-date [purses only]) X (Number of races started) / 1,000

The problem with this one was that by winning a big purse, for example, at Daytona, the effects of that one purse would be multiplied every time you entered a race, regardless of

where you finished. Winners of races actually ended up losing points to drivers finishing behind them.

1975: Bob Latford is a walking encyclopedia of NASCAR lore, having worked in NASCAR since the 1950s—in the mail room, as a publicist, in public relations, and even once as the pace car driver. He'll likely be best remembered, though, as the man who invented the current Winston Cup points scheme. First used in the 1975 season, the system rewards consistent top finishes and is universally applied at all tracks and events.

Points are awarded based on the finishing position:

• 1st place: 175 points
• 2nd through 5th place: 170–155, dropping by 5 points
• 6th through 10th place: 150–138, dropping by 4 points
• 11th place back: 137 down, dropping by 3 points
• If you don't start a race, you get 0 points.
• 5 bonus points are awarded to any driver who leads at least one lap in a race
• 5 bonus points are awarded to the driver who leads the most laps in the race.

The system rewards drivers for finishing up front—the sliding scale gets a team progressively more points the higher it finishes. Hard running is encouraged by the bonuses to the lap leaders. The only complaint so far has been that there is no bonus for winning a race, other than the five bonus points for leading the last lap. This means that drivers with consistent top-five finishes can take the championship over drivers who win a lot but also finish poorly in many races.

OPPOSITE: *The state of Dale Earnhardt's #3 and Tim Richmond's #25 cars is characteristic of their 1986 rough-and-tumble season. Richmond struggled through crashes and breakdowns in the first half of the year while Earnhardt was losing sheet metal but gaining positions on his way to his second championship.* BELOW: *The point system now in use requires a driver to start a race to earn points. Drivers in competition for the championship cannot afford to miss even one event, which has led many drivers to strap themselves in the car the week after bone-breaking crashes. Here Bobby Labonte is helped from his car in the 1999 TransSouth 400 at Darlington after breaking his shoulder blade two days earlier. He made the requisite laps and scored the points earned by the relief driver.*

ABOVE: *This was one of the few superspeedway races David Pearson did not win in 1973. The #21 Mercury sat on the pole for the National 500 at Charlotte but was collected along with Darrell Waltrip when Charlie Glotzbach's Pylon #28 spun in front of them.*
LEFT: *Bobby Allison contemplates the view from his office. Allison started the 1974 season in his own Chevys but moved to the Penske Matadors in mid-season, earning two wins for the team that year.*

1974: Same Old, Same Old—
Petty Makes It Five

Amid the upheaval of the OPEC oil embargo, NASCAR continued to make changes to the points system and engine rules in an ongoing effort to broaden competition. The year 1974 saw perhaps the most peculiar points system used in the Winston Cup. Points were calculated based on finishing position multiplied by money won so far that year. With this system, a driver could finish ahead of a competitor over the course of the year but still lose points to him. Indeed, with large dollar wins like Daytona, Petty was able to gain points throughout the season and win the championship, even though Yarborough led him in most categories—including number of wins and laps and races led. Even though David Pearson competed in only nineteen of thirty events, he was able to place third in the points standing. Even worse, no one (drivers or fans) understood how the points worked. Another revamp was guaranteed for 1975.

Despite the changes, the season was thoroughly dominated by three drivers—Petty, Yarborough, and Pearson—who among them won the first twenty-seven of thirty events. Of the last three, Yarborough's Carling teammate won one, while Bobby Allison ran a combination of his own Chevys and Roger Penske's Matadors, getting one win in each of the remaining two. Although R.J. Reynolds continued to put additional money into the sport, it was obvious that only teams with backing from major sponsors could really compete at the top. Petty had STP, Pearson had Purolator, and Yarborough had Kar-Kare and Carling Beer, which gave Junior Johnson sufficient funds to allow him to buy full ownership of the #11 team from Richard Howard. Otherwise, there were few big-money sponsors, and thus few other serious competitors.

Darrell Waltrip's association with Bud Moore hadn't worked out as well as either had hoped and was not renewed for 1974. Waltrip ran his own #95 team, and Moore brought in Canadian road-racer George Follmer, an old friend from Moore's SCCA days. (It didn't hurt that Follmer brought the RC Cola sponsorship with him.) Follmer didn't get the results Moore was looking for either, though, and by May the Canadian was replaced by Buddy Baker, who was out of the K&K Insurance ride when Krauskopf yanked the team yet again, to protest the rules changes.

Highlights of the season included Petty's fifth Daytona victory, in a race that, shortened in response to the fuel crisis, actually started on lap 20. Donnie Allison, driving for the new #88 DiGard team, almost pulled off an upset victory, only to lose the lead when a tire blew with just eleven

1973 Championship Standings

Place	Car#	Driver	Car Type	Points
1	72	Benny Parsons	Chevy	7173.80
2	11	Cale Yarborough	Chevy	7106.65
3	24	Cecil Gordon	Chevy	7046.80
4	48	James Hylton	Chevy	6972.75
5	43	Richard Petty	Dodge	6877.95
6	71	Buddy Baker	Dodge	6327.60
7	12	Bobby Allison	Chevy	6272.60
8	30	Walter Ballard	Mercury	5955.70
9	64	Elmo Langley	Ford	5826.85
10	70	J.D. McDuffie	Chevy	5743.90

laps to go. Nevertheless, the team put on a good show through the year, earning a place in the top twenty in points in their first year together.

By July, the races were back to full length. Petty picked up the win in Winston Cup's first race at the Pocono, Pennsylvania, track in August. The race at Talladega was eventful, as always. Before the race, sabotage was detected in as many as twenty cars, including those of all the leading teams. The investigation concluded that it was an inside job, but no suspects were ever named.

Darrell Waltrip made a strong showing in the fall Southern 500, coming in second to Cale Yarborough, in a race that had only twelve cars left running at the end. The rest of the field, including most of the other season contenders, was eliminated in the numerous crashes or by mechanical problems.

Earl Ross, a Canadian rookie in Johnson's second team car, won a surprise victory at Martinsville in September after the leader, teammate Cale Yarborough, dropped out. Despite a respectable first year, however, Ross would find his ride in jeopardy at season's end. Carling had signed on with Johnson for a four-year sponsorship, but when it became clear late in the year that Yarborough would not win the championship they pulled the plug on the deal. Johnson was left dumbfounded and once again in search of a sponsor.

1974 Championship Standings

Place	Car#	Driver	Car Type	Points
1	43	Richard Petty	Dodge	5037.750
2	11	Cale Yarborough	Chevy	4470.300
3	21	David Pearson	Mercury	2389.250
4	12	Bobby Allison	Matador	2019.195
5	72	Benny Parsons	Ford	1591.500
6	2/71	Dave Marcis	Dodge	1378.200
7	71/15	Buddy Baker	Dodge/Ford	1016.880
8	52	Earl Ross	Chevy	1009.470
9	24	Cecil Gordon	Chevy	1000.650
10	05	David Sisco	Chevy	956.200

PREVIOUS PAGES: *Check out those pants! Bill and Jim Gardner and Mike DiProspero formed the DiGard team in 1973. Donnie Allison was named as their driver. The #08 crew pits here during the 1973 Winston 500.* LEFT: *There was once another Gordon who drove the #24 car. Cecil Gordon ran his own team from 1970 through 1983. Here his Chevy leads L.D. Ottinger's #02 car in 1974.* ABOVE: *The STP Dodge continued to dominate the course in 1974.*

Junior Johnson: From Winning Driver to Winning Owner

to bringing Johnson another championship trophy in 1992, but—in the closest race in NASCAR history—finished ten points behind Alan Kulwicki. Johnson's skill as an owner and mechanic, his savvy selection of drivers, and his willingness to push the limits of the rules have combined to make him the winningest owner in NASCAR's modern era.

It would be hard to overstate Junior Johnson's contribution to NASCAR racing. Called "The Last American Hero" by writer Tom Wolfe, Robert "Junior" Johnson got his first racing lessons as a moonshine driver in the hills of North Carolina. He drove his first NASCAR race in 1953 and got his first win the same year; in his thirteen-year driving career, he won fifty races. Johnson earned his reputation as one of the toughest, hardest-charging drivers ever.

Johnson moved from driver to team owner in 1966, teaming up with LeeRoy Yarbrough; their #98 Fords would win nearly everything in sight over the next three years. When Ford withdrew from racing in 1970, Johnson almost dropped out. He sold his Ford equipment and started a Chevy team with backing from financier Richard Howard in 1971.

Bobby Allison brought Coca-Cola sponsorship to the team the next year, and Johnson soon returned to victory lane. He bought out Howard in 1974, and fielded two cars with Earl Ross and Cale Yarborough as drivers. Yarborough, Darrell Waltrip, Neil Bonnett, and Terry Labonte drove for Junior over the next fifteen years, with Waltrip and Bonnett as members of a two-car team through the mid-1980s. Yarborough and Waltrip each won three championships for Johnson, in 1976, 1977, 1978, 1981, 1982, and 1985.

In 1990, Johnson went back to two teams, with Geoff Bodine and Sterling Marlin as drivers. Bill Elliott came close

LEFT: *Johnson treats the fans to a smile in the winners circle with Cale Yarborough and crew chief Herb Nab in 1973 after winning the National 500 at Charlotte.*
ABOVE: *Before the days of color-coordinated team uniforms, Johnson tracks lap times for Cale Yarborough at North Wilkesboro in September 1974. The times were probably pretty good—the team won the race, one of ten victories that year.*
RIGHT: *Johnson's success as a team owner was due in part to his hands-on approach. His race-day pit crew duty was to supply the tire changer with the new tires. Crew chief Herb Nab mans the air wrench for the #11 team here in 1974.*

Chapter Two

Sponsorship Brings Stability: 1975 to 1979

By the end of 1974, NASCAR had become a study in contrasts. Winston advertising dollars and the performances of drivers like Richard Petty and Cale Yarborough were attracting more and more fans to the sport. No longer just filling the stands, NASCAR had been discovered by network TV and was reaching potential fans across the country. RJR remained committed to the Winston Cup, and the sport as a whole looked healthy and seemed likely to continue thriving.

When you drilled down and looked at the status of the individual teams, though, you got a different picture. While the WC points funds were attractive, most teams didn't have enough money to build and field a car to earn those points. Without factory-provided parts, the cost of running a race team was prohibitively high. By 1975, Cotton Owens, Holman-Moody, Mario Rossi, and others had closed shop. Last-minute financing from Richard Howard rescued Junior Johnson, but the team continued to struggle. Another source of funding was needed.

What had kept some of the teams in the black since 1970 was money provided by corporate sponsors. Since NASCAR's earliest days, the shiny expanse of stock cars'

rear fenders had sported company logos, often the name of the owner's garage or a local car dealership like Smokey Yunick's "Best Damn Garage in Town." By the early 1970s, a number of large companies had made the natural association between auto racing and automotive products. The cars became "rolling billboards," promoting the products by virtue of the car's performance. Several of the top teams negotiated sponsorship deals that would bring funding to the teams when they needed it—up front or week to week. Bobby Allison had benefited from Coca-Cola sponsorship, which had given him the leverage to switch teams as he pleased. After testing the waters with Fred Lorenzen's car the previous year, STP moved to Richard Petty's in 1972, starting the longest team-sponsor relationship in the sport's history. Purolator oil filters hooked up with David Pearson in 1971 and followed him to the Wood Brothers team in 1972.

Other teams were less fortunate. Many sponsors rushed onto the scene with little understanding of the sport or its potential, only to pull out when their car didn't immediately win a championship. Bud Moore lost his RC Cola backing, and Junior Johnson, all smiles with major funding from Carling Brewery, was shocked when they suddenly pulled out of their three-year deal at the end of 1974.

NASCAR and RJR stepped in to help. In 1975, the Awards and Achievement Plan paid what amounted to appearance money to four teams (Johnson, Moore, Petty, and K&K)—$3,000 for superspeedway events and $2,000 for short tracks. Other teams in the top twenty in points could earn smaller sums. Additional assistance came from Goodyear, in the form of free tires. On superspeedways, 144 tires were given to the top twelve qualifiers; a smaller number was distributed at short tracks.

While these measures, and the growth of the WC points fund, helped pay the bills, it still wasn't enough to keep the teams going for long. Over the course of the second half of the 1970s, an upswing in corporate interest in NASCAR did the trick. And while RJR's continued involvement contributed to this trend, the driving force (so to speak) was television.

NASCAR Comes to the Small Screen

NASCAR had entered into a contract with ABC Sports as early as 1969. The network planned to broadcast highlights of nine races in 1970, with portions of several shown live. The broadcasts drew surprisingly good ratings, and ABC expanded its coverage in 1975. A second network, CBS, got into the mix in 1975, airing tape-delayed broadcasts of Talladega and the World 600 in their entirety.

With major coverage from two networks, NASCAR began to attract attention in corporate boardrooms as a solid advertising opportunity—and not just for oil companies and car parts manufacturers. The DiGard team, with Darrell Waltrip at the wheel, acquired major sponsorship from Gatorade in 1975. Holly Farms renewed its association with Junior Johnson, helping to pull that team back from the brink yet again. Gradually, through the remainder of the decade, a wider variety of companies tied their names to more and more race teams.

PAGE 54: *Benny Parsons lost a half-lap lead over Cale Yarborough when he ran out of gas and had to coast to the pits in the 1977 National 500 at Charlotte. He came out behind the #11, but floored the accelerator and passed Cale on lap 297.*
PAGE 55: *Janet Guthrie was certainly not the first woman to compete in NASCAR, but because of her Indy car association (and canny promotion by Humpy Wheeler at Charlotte) she was perhaps the most widely known. Guthrie, with sponsorship from Kelly Girl, made a run at Rookie of the Year in 1977 but lost to Ricky Rudd. Janet logged several races in 1978 and 1980 and ended her NASCAR career with five top-five finishes.*
RIGHT: *Donnie Allison pits the DiGard #88 in the Atlanta 500 in March 1975. He finished fourth in the race, but lost the ride in August to the up-and-coming Darrell Waltrip.*

RIGHT: *Bobby Allison said he was just trying to separate brother Donnie and Cale Yarborough, but he ended up in the midst of the action in the infield at the end of the 1979 Daytona 500. CBS, which televised the race, and the fight, saw the ratings jump from an already high 10.5 (about 16 million viewers) to 13.5 for the last half hour. CBS execs said they were "very, very pleased" by the show. NASCAR execs were less enthusiastic.*
BELOW: *Dave Marcis had his most successful seasons with the Nord Krauskopf #71 team, in 1975 and 1976. Here he's trailed closely by Benny Parsons in the L.G. DeWitt #72 Chevy.*

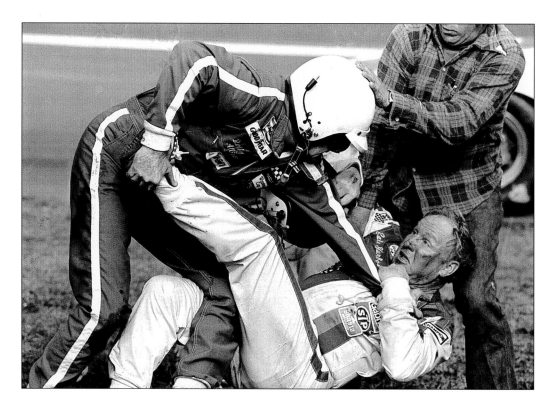

A Tale of Two Daytonas A recent magazine poll asked race fans to identify the most memorable moments in NASCAR history. Most of the responses involved the Daytona Speedway, and of those responses two Daytona 500s in particular showed up at the top of the list.

Encouraged by its ratings the previous year, ABC decided to broadcast the end of the 1976 Daytona 500 live for the first time. The closing laps set a scene familiar to race fans—David Pearson and Richard Petty nose-to-tail, fighting for the win. But there was more in store for the home viewers than a close finish. On the last lap, Pearson shot past Petty on the backstretch to take the lead, but slid up high in turn three. Petty was able to pull back up beside him. When they hit turn four, they literally hit turn four: the cars touched and Pearson turned into the wall, sending Petty into the wall as well. The wreck carried onto the front stretch and left the #43 stalled on the track, just shy of the finish line. The #21 sat in the infield, its front end smashed, but with the engine still running. While Petty tried to restart his car, Pearson's Purolator Mercury limped through the grass and across the finish line for the win.

Suddenly NASCAR was news. The replay made sports highlights segments across the country, and people who had never even heard of stock car racing were now choosing favorites between two of NASCAR's superstars.

The 1979 Daytona 500 provided an even more spectacular "made for TV" finish. Cale Yarborough and Donnie Allison were fighting for the lead, with Petty a distant third. Yarborough ducked under Allison's #1 on the backstretch on the final lap. Allison moved over to block the pass and the two cars came together. As they went through turn three they slammed into each other

repeatedly, finally spinning down to the bottom of the track. Yarborough, who felt that Allison had been a little too aggressive, climbed out of his car to express his feelings on the matter—with his fists. With an ice storm blanketing much of the Northeast, the broadcast had drawn a huge audience, who now saw Yarborough, Donnie Allison, and Bobby Allison (who had stopped to check on his brother) slug it out on the grass while Petty slipped by in amazement to win his sixth 500.

Although NASCAR officially decried the incident and fined the participants, it was one of the biggest publicity draws in the sport's history.

A New Champion A number of teams made strong showings through the second half of the 1970s. Dave Marcis took over the K&K #71 ride in 1975, earning four wins and second place in the points standings. Buddy Baker had moved into Bud Moore's Fords and picked up five wins with him, while Darrell Waltrip was making a name for himself driving for the DiGard team (with Gatorade sponsorship), giving fans a glimpse of what was in store for the next decade. Waltrip moved steadily up in the points standings, showing championship potential with twenty wins between 1975 to 1979.

Nevertheless, Petty, Pearson, Allison, and Yarborough were still the biggest names in stock car racing and the top contenders for the title.

Pearson and the Wood Brothers were a team made in heaven, but they never ran the full schedule, so although they captured more than their share of wins, they were never really in the run for a championship. Bobby Allison, first with Roger Penske, then with his own team, then with

The remains of Tiny Lund's #26 Dodge are towed to the garage after a crash at Talladega in August 1975. Lund, forty-two at the time, spun his car on the back-stretch in the sixth lap of the race and was killed when Terry Link ran into him. Link himself almost died, sitting unconscious in his burning car until two spectators jumped the fence to rescue him.

Bud Moore, couldn't achieve the consistency he needed to vie for the top spot.

Petty's success with his Dodge Charger continued in the 1974 and 1975 championships, but the competition was much stronger in 1976. Yarborough's #11 swept the short tracks, while Pearson was unbeatable on the super-speedways. Petty, recovering from major surgery for stomach ulcers in the off-season, was held to just three wins that year. The Petty team, suffering from mechanical problems and an aging car design, didn't fare much better in 1977. When the Charger was officially retired by NASCAR as a legitimate model in 1978, Petty moved over to the new Chrysler product, the Dodge Magnum, a car with the same connotations for race fans as the Edsel has for marketing pundits. Underpowered, difficult to handle on the superspeedways, and prone to mechanical problems, the Magnum never performed well, either for Petty or for the other teams that used it. Petty suffered five DNFs ("did not finish") in the first six races of 1978.

By July, when it had become clear that Chrysler was no longer committed to making their model competitive, Petty decided to end his family's long association with the manufacturer. Petty moved to GM and raced Chevys for the rest of the year. The change didn't pay off immediately, but by the end of the next season—racing a combination of Chevys, Oldsmobiles, and Buicks—Petty was able to come from behind and beat Waltrip for the 1979 championship, his seventh.

The Junior Johnson and Cale Yarborough team had threatened to win a title for several years, finishing second in 1973 and 1974, but then experienced a disappointing 1975 season. By 1976, though, with Holly Farms as a sponsor and Petty faltering, Yarborough's time had come. The team dominated the short tracks that year with nine wins. Pearson tried to play the spoiler, taking ten wins, but Johnson and Yarborough had done well enough overall for the #11 to earn its first championship. The team was solid again in 1977, and, despite challenges on and off the track from Darrell Waltrip (they had taken to verbally sparring beween races), Yarborough was able once again to capture nine wins and take home the championship.

Despite their strong performances in 1976 and 1977, the #11 team was actually considered the underdog for the 1978 season—up to that point, no one had ever won three championships in a row. In addition, the team was working with a new sponsor and a new crew chief, Tim Brewer. But Brewer was working out well, and the team was able to focus on winning races and the championship. It helped that competitors Petty and Waltrip were distracted by car difficulties (Petty's Magnum) and team reshuffling (the revolving door of personnel changes at DiGard). Yarborough went on to ten wins and the three-peat, which at this writing remains a unique feat.

End of an Era for Chrysler

Richard Petty had put Chrysler at the top of the charts in stock car racing. He had been riding the Dodge Charger since the Superbird went by the wayside in 1970, and had won three championships with it. Although the Charger was one of Petty's favorite race cars, by 1977 the model had run its course. NASCAR's mandate for smaller engines would have required inordinately expensive modifications.

In 1978, Chrysler released a new model to replace the Charger. The Dodge Magnum's aerodynamics and power didn't come close to the Charger's, however, and "the rolling brick" was Chrysler's swan song in NASCAR. Several teams struggled with the car through the season, but by the end of the year almost all finally switched to GM out of desperation. Chrysler was effectively out of stock car racing.

General Motors fared better with the rules changes. They were a step ahead of the competition with their small block engine, and the new Chevy Laguna had a sleek front end with good aerodynamics. To level the field, NASCAR mandated use of a restrictor plate on the Chevy engine, but GM was making the same engine available for all of its models. This meant that teams had some options. For example, a team could run the same engine in Oldsmobiles and Buicks without incurring a penalty. Many teams elected to run the unencumbered Olds on the superspeedway and the Chevy on the short tracks. Petty found new success with this formula, while NASCAR, happy to have several car makes represented on the track, left the situation alone. Meanwhile, Ford teams could choose between the Thunderbird and the Mercury.

OPPOSITE TOP: *Before adopting the #71 for his own team, Dave Marcis drove for the K&K #71 crew (K&K was a racetrack insurance company). In 1975, the team returned to NASCAR full-time with Marcis and crew chief Harry Hyde.*
OPPOSITE BOTTOM: *Richard Childress is best known as the owner of Dale Earnhardt's #3 team, but for many years he raced the #3 Chevy himself. From 1969 to 1981 Childress raced on a limited budget. Note the working conditions in the "garage" area in this 1976 race—a far cry from today's high-tech haulers and garage bays.*

The Wood Brothers

Glen and Leonard Wood began their long association with NASCAR—and with the #21—in 1953, with Glen at the wheel and Leonard as mechanic. Over the next ten years, the brothers would race in the Grand National and convertible divisions and on the modified circuit. When Ford reentered Grand National racing in 1962, Glen climbed out of the seat, and the two sponsored Marvin Panch as driver. Tiny Lund subbed for an injured Panch in 1963 and, relying on the Woods' unique emphasis on fast pit stops, won the Daytona 500.

Cale Yarborough, Donnie Allison, and A.J. Foyt drove the #21 Mercurys through the 1960s. In 1972, David Pearson joined the team and began a storybook seven-year period, accumulating fifty-three wins and dominating the competition on the superspeedways.

Pearson left in 1979, after a misunderstanding in the pit cost the team a win, and was replaced by Neil Bonnett. Buddy Baker followed, then Kyle Petty in a #7 Ford. Returning to #21 several seasons later, Neil Bonnett rejoined the team until he was injured in 1990. Dale Jarrett picked up the reins, and was followed by Morgan Shepherd, Michael Waltrip, and Elliot Sadler (in 1999).

Just as the brothers have sponsored several second-generation drivers, the leadership of the #21 team has of late moved more and more to second-generation Woods. Glen's sons Eddie and Len will undoubtedly carry on the Wood Brothers' tradition of excellence through the next twenty years of NASCAR racing.

LEFT: *David Pearson had a good chance to win his first race of 1979 at the Rebel 300 at Darlington until he tried to return to the race with only two tires. The tires remained on pit road as he drove away. The #21 team wasn't the only one having pit troubles that day—Yarborough ran out of gas twice during the race.*
ABOVE: *Pearson did score one win that year, filling in for an injured Dale Earnhardt in the Osterlund #2 car. Pearson celebrates his win in the Southern 500.*

1975: Petty Unchallenged in a Year of Transition

As drivers were adjusting to the new engine rules, Petty had his Charger in fighting trim and was ready to go after his sixth championship. Though the usual competitors were back, Petty, with no serious challengers, wrapped up the title with several races to go.

Pearson and the Wood Brothers had another strong season in 1975, with three superspeedway wins. Cale Yarborough had three wins, too, but wasn't consistent enough to challenge for the title. Bobby Allison was driving Roger Penske's Matadors, but Penske would run only a partial schedule, taking Allison out of contention as well. Benny Parsons in the L.G. DeWitt #72 put together another solid year, finishing fourth in the points.

Buddy Baker hooked up with Bud Moore's #15 Ford team for the year. Although Moore had to rely for funding on one-race sponsorship deals, often put together at the last minute by track promoters, the team won four races—including the last two races of the year—running a partial schedule. The finale was especially exciting. The #15 wasn't scheduled to run the season finisher at Ontario, but Moore landed a sponsorship from Norris Industries at the eleventh hour and Norris wanted to see its car run. The team entered at the last minute, and the sponsor must have been pleased to see its white and blue Ford sitting in victory lane at the end of the race.

Nord Krauskopf had been feuding with NASCAR over rules changes for years, pulling his #71 team out, then coming back when the rules were more favorable to his car. The 1975 season was an "in" season, and Krauskopf had Dave Marcis in the ride with Harry Hyde as crew chief. Marcis got his first career win at Martinsville, his brakes outlasting second-place Parsons, on the short track. Marcis put together sixteen top-fives and was Petty's closest competition for the title, finishing second.

1975 Championship Standings

Place	Car#	Driver	Car Type	Points
1	43	Richard Petty	Dodge	4,783
2	71	Dave Marcis	Dodge	4,061
3	48	James Hylton	Chevy	3,914
4	72	Benny Parsons	Chevy	3,820
5	3	Richard Childress	Chevy	3,818
6	24	Cecil Gordon	Chevy	3,702
7	17/88	Darrell Waltrip	Chevy	3,462
8	64	Elmo Langley	Ford	3,399
9	11	Cale Yarborough	Chevy	3,295
10	90	Dick Brooks	Ford	3,182

Buddy Baker and Valvoline joined the Wood Brothers' team in 1983. Leonard Wood, in sponsor livery, chats with former teammate David Pearson. Pearson (aka "The Silver Fox") formed his own team (#16) with Chattanooga Chew tobacco as the sponsor. In 1985 the Wood Brothers changed car numbers (#7 for Kyle Petty's 7-Eleven sponsorship) and Pearson reclaimed the #21 for his own car.

Darrell Waltrip made the move that vaulted him into the NASCAR spotlight, replacing Donnie Allison in the DiGard #88. Waltrip had won his first race early in the year, and was tapped when Allison was dismissed in August. The winless DiGard team didn't have to wait long for victory—Waltrip visited the winner's circle again at Richmond in October, coming from three laps behind for the win.

On a sad note, popular racer DeWayne "Tiny" Lund was killed in the August Talladega race. Lund, returning to Winston Cup competition after a two-year absence, spun his car into the grass early in the race. Rookie driver Terry Link lost control, and T-boned Lund on the driver's side, killing him instantly. Buddy Baker, a close friend of Lund's, won the race. When told of Lund's death, Baker dropped to his knees in anguish in victory lane.

1976: Yarborough Finally Takes the Championship

The 1976 season started out with a bang. After Pearson captured the opener at Riverside, the circuit moved to Daytona. The weekend's excitement started with the qualifying race, when Darrell Waltrip, Dave Marcis, and A.J. Foyt (in Hoss Elington's #28) drove laps at speeds of between 185 and 187mph (298 and 301kph) while everyone else mysteriously ran below 183 (294kph). Many drivers cited "fouled spark plugs," "ignition problems," and other mechanical ills for their slower laps. The situation was suspect, and NASCAR stepped in with an "or else" inspection of the three fast cars. Following considerable deliberation and legal counsel, NASCAR disallowed their qualifying times after finding questionable fuel lines, perhaps linked to speed-boosting nitrous oxide bottles. The use of nitrous would explain the faster-than-average laps, but why was everyone else slower than normal? According to Ed Negre, owner of the #8 car, a group of drivers conspired to run slower than usual so the suspected cheaters would stand out clearly to NASCAR officials. Ironically, Negre would later be fined for using nitrous oxide himself.

All of this resulted in a strange front row for the Daytona race, with Canadian Ramo Stott next to rookie Terry Ryan in the latter's first Winston Cup race. And that was just the beginning. Broadcast live on ABC, the 1976 Daytona 500 featured a slam-bang finish, with Petty and Pearson colliding on the last lap and Pearson coaxing his battered car over the finish line past a stalled #43.

The rest of the season was all Cale Yarborough and David Pearson. Petty climbed out of a hospital bed after stomach surgery to make the Riverside date, but was

Cale Yarborough (and a buddy) relax in the winner's circle after taking the 1978 Southern 500. It was Cale's fourth win in the historic race. The win was secured with pit strategy. With thirty-two laps to go, Darrell Waltrip pitted for tires. Yarborough followed him in but took only gas and beat him out onto the track.

1976 Championship Standings

Place	Car#	Driver	Car Type	Points
1	11	Cale Yarborough	Chevy	4,644
2	43	Richard Petty	Dodge	4,449
3	72	Benny Parsons	Chevy	4,304
4	2	Bobby Allison	Mercury	4,097
5	54	Lennie Pond	Chevy	3,930
6	71	Dave Marcis	Dodge	3,875
7	15	Buddy Baker	Ford	3,745
8	88	Darrell Waltrip	Chevy	3,505
9	21	David Pearson	Mercury	3,483
10	90	Dick Brooks	Ford	3,447

Cale Yarborough

Yarborough's story is one of those amazing American rags-to-riches tales. From a humble beginning in South Carolina, Cale Yarborough rose to become one of the greatest stock car racers in history. Known for his toughness and strength of will, Yarborough endured some tough times before his break in NASCAR came along. Once he got that break, though, Cale was unstoppable. By 1972 he had driven for such top teams as Holman-Moody and the Wood Brothers. In 1968, Yarborough had a banner year, with six wins in the Wood Brothers #21 Mercury. When Ford pulled its factory backing in 1970, Yarborough left the Wood Brothers for a go at the Indy car circuit.

In 1973, Yarborough hooked up with Junior Johnson and Richard Howard's team, with a former mechanic by the name of Robert Yates building engines for their Chevys. The team immediately took off, posting four wins in their first season together. Johnson, who took over full ownership of the team

in 1974, guided Cale and the #11 to three consecutive Winston Cup championships, in 1976, 1977, and 1978.

In 1981, Yarborough moved on to the #27 team of millionaire M.C. Anderson, who was gunning for his own championship and felt Yarborough was the driver to achieve it. By then, however, Yarborough was committed to spending more time with his family and would race only a portion of the schedule. Although the team did well, earning five wins, Anderson was adamant that they go for the championship full-time in 1983. He is said to have offered Yarborough $1 million up front to drive full-time for him; when Yarborough refused, Anderson's disappointment was such that he closed down his team rather than continue with another driver.

Yarborough moved on to Harry Ranier's #28 Hardee's team, driving Chevys, then Fords, through 1986, when he made the jump to running his own team, driving his own Olds through the 1988 season. Yarborough, fifth on the all-time NASCAR win list, continues as an owner today, running the #98 Ford team.

Yarborough ran with the Ranier-Lundy team between 1983 and 1986. The Hardee's Ford failed to finish the 1985 Nationwide 500 at Rockingham when Cale spun the car on lap 390, also taking out Lake Speed in the Rahmoc #75 and Tommy Ellis's #18 car.

subpar for the whole year. Dave Marcis, returning with the #71, picked up three wins but finished sixth in points. Allison and Penske switched from Matadors to Fords after early problems with the AMCs that year. And although they finished fourth in the standings, they were winless for the year.

Pearson wrapped up most of the superspeedway wins, while Yarborough in the Holly Farms #11 captured nine races, most on short tracks. Yarborough and Johnson's performance was strong enough to lead them to their first Winston Cup championship.

There had been a number of female drivers in NASCAR in the 1940s and 1950s, but no women raced in the Winston Cup until 1976, when the new Charlotte Speedway vice president H.A. "Humpy" Wheeler brought

Janet Guthrie to the World 600. With a background in sports cars, Guthrie was looking to move up to big-league racing. Unable to qualify for the Indy 500, she came to Charlotte and four other Winston Cup races to try stock car racing instead. She finished a respectable fifteenth at Charlotte and would return in 1977 to try for Rookie of the Year honors.

1977: *Two in a Row*

The next year was more of the same for Yarborough and Junior Johnson. Despite strong words at times between driver and owner concerning the strength of the car, they pulled together for nine wins and a repeat of the championship. Yarborough also scored the most Winston Cup

points ever recorded—5,000—since the 1975 points structure had been put in place.

Wins at Nashville and Pocono helped Benny Parsons, in his eighth season with L.G. DeWitt, to third place in the standings. Dave Marcis left the K&K ride to go to work for Roger Penske. When K&K decided to finally close shop, Kentucky coal miner Jim Stacy bought the team,

BELOW: *Hoss Ellington worked with many of the big-name drivers in the 1970s and 1980s. Donnie Allison joined the team in 1975 and remained into the 1980 season. They were able to score only three wins, though, and Ellington replaced Allison with David Pearson in 1980. Here Allison follows Buddy Baker at Charlotte in 1977.* RIGHT: *Darrell Waltrip hit full stride with the DiGard team in the late 1970s. The relationship was fruitful but turbulent. Waltrip later summed it up as, "They didn't like me and I didn't like them."*

1977 Championship Standings

Place	Car#	Driver	Car Type	Points
1	11	Cale Yarborough	Chevy	5,000
2	43	Richard Petty	Dodge	4,614
3	72	Benny Parsons	Chevy	4,570
4	88	Darrell Waltrip	Chevy	4,498
5	15	Buddy Baker	Ford	3,961
6	90	Dick Brooks	Ford	3,742
7	48	James Hylton	Chevy	3,476
8	12	Bobby Allison	Matador	3,467
9	3	Richard Childress	Chevy	3,463
10	24	Cecil Gordon	Chevy	3,294

changed the number from 71 to 5, and put Neil Bonnett in the ride. The team came up with two wins. Donnie Allison hooked up with Hoss Ellington and sponsor Hawaiian Tropic, and the #1 team won at Talladega and Rockingham.

Bobby Allison gave up the Penske seat because of the team's lack of competitiveness the previous year, and fielded his own Matadors. In a final echo from an earlier era, AMC provided factory backing for his operation.

Darrell Waltrip had his best year yet with six wins and a fourth-place standing, in spite of conflict within the #88 team that resulted from DiGard's efforts to land a championship lineup. Darel Dieringer was hired as team coordinator in April, and a month later crew chief David Ifft left. After a dry spell for the team, Buddy Parrott was hired as crew chief and Dieringer was let go.

Yarborough and Pearson lead the field to the green flag at Atlanta Raceway in 1978. Scoring confusion in the final laps led to confusion at the finish: first Donnie Allison was awarded the win, but then it was awarded to Richard Petty. Ultimately, Allison was given the victor's laurel. The angle of this photo emphasizes the size of the Winston Cup cars at that time—years before downsizing hit the series.

1978: Cale Makes History

There were changes in a number of teams in 1978. The previous year had been the last one in which 1974 models were still eligible, so many of the teams found themselves dealing with new makes for the first time in a while. In Richard Petty's case, this proved nothing less than disastrous. Petty moved from the faithful Dodge Charger to the Magnum, which he abandoned in desperation in mid-season, switching to GM and ending a long relationship with Chrysler. Even after the change Petty struggled, finishing sixth in the points, with no wins.

Bobby Allison moved to Bud Moore's team, replacing Buddy Baker, who had gone to M.C. Anderson's #27. The team switched from Mercury Montegos to Ford T-Birds and were immediately successful. They got their first Daytona 500 win (breaking a long winless streak for both) and four more victories for the season, enough to place them second in points.

Californian Rod Osterlund formed a new team with Dave Marcis as driver. Marcis had become available when Roger Penske pulled out of NASCAR racing completely after the 1977 season. Jim Stacy's team returned intact—for a while at least. Before the season was over, crew chief Harry Hyde filed suit against Stacy for nonpayment of

Chesapeake, Virgina, racer Ricky Rudd first hit Winston Cup in 1975. From 1976 through 1978 he drove Chevys, Fords, and Buicks fielded by his father, Al Rudd. The team had no wins and few top finishes, but Ricky had the chance to show his potential, attracting the attention of the DiGard team in 1981 (when it was in search of a replacement for the departing Waltrip).

1978 Championship Standings

Place	Car#	Driver	Car Type	Points
1	11	Cale Yarborough	Olds	4,841
2	15	Bobby Allison	Ford	4,367
3	88	Darrell Waltrip	Chevy	4,362
4	72	Benny Parsons	Chevy	4,350
5	2	Dave Marcis	Chevy	4,335
6	43	Richard Petty	Dodge/Chevy	3,949
7	54	Lennie Pond	Chevy	3,794
8	90	Dick Brooks	Mercury	3,769
9	67	Buddy Arrington	Dodge	3,626
10	3	Richard Childress	Chevy	3,566

bills, and the shop was padlocked by court order. Neil Bonnett ended up in cars leased from Osterlund's shop.

Pearson and the Wood Brothers, though not as dominant as in previous years, still won four races, including Pearson's one-hundredth career victory at Rockingham. Harry Ranier's was another new team, with Lennie Pond driving the #54 Chevys and Olds. The team scored a victory at Talladega but split up over internal differences at the end of the year.

Speaking of internal differences, the ongoing soap opera with the DiGard team was renewed for another season. Amid other personnel changes, Waltrip announced that he wanted out of his contract so that he could join Harry Ranier's team in 1979. DiGard's Bill Gardner at first put Waltrip's contract up for bid, but later insisted that it would be honored, by court order if necessary. In a surprise announcement in October, the two indicated that they'd worked out their differences, and Waltrip would remain with the team. Again, despite the fuss, they had a great year—six wins and third place in the points standings. The team had become a contender to win each race.

The #11 team remained focused and on track. Cale Yarborough romped to ten wins, taking the points lead from Benny Parsons in June and never looking back.

Yarborough and Johnson hit the history books with their third consecutive championship.

There were also changes at the NASCAR tracks this year, most notably a transition in ownership at Bristol International Speedway. The new owners were committed to improvements and planned to add new stands and box seating. They increased their Winston Cup races to five hundred laps each and scheduled the autumn race to run on Saturday night under lights.

The Winston Cup took another big step toward national recognition in 1978, when President Jimmy Carter invited a group of NASCAR VIPs to the White House. A crowd of drivers, owners, sponsors, promoters, and media reps gathered for an evening of entertainment on the White House lawn with First Lady Rosalynn Carter presiding.

1979: Petty Returns to Form

Having won their third straight championship the previous year, Cale and Junior were back together in 1979 trying for a fourth—but sporting new colors. When Citibank pulled its sponsorship from the #11 and the #72 teams, Johnson brought on Busch beer. The defending champs were able to muster only four wins and a fourth-place finish in the points, however, due to the high level of competition that year.

Two teams fought for the title, one still on its way up and the other making a comeback. Richard Petty again spent the off-season in the hospital for stomach ulcers, getting off a gurney and into a race car for the Riverside opener. Unlike the previous year, the team had had enough time with their new GM machines to work out the kinks and was back in contention.

The team that Petty battled was DiGard's #88. In a year of relative calm for that crew, they took the points lead right from the first race and, with six wins, held it for almost the whole year. Petty fought back from a 229-point deficit in August and, with two races remaining, took the lead from Waltrip. Waltrip recaptured it the next week, and they went into the last race only two points apart. Both drivers ran near the front from the start of the race, but on lap 38 Waltrip spun his car to avoid a wreck in front of him and had to pit for tires. He was caught in the pits, went a lap down to Petty, and never made it up. Richard Petty won his seventh championship in the last

OPPOSITE: *Miller Beer has been one of the biggest sponsors in Winston Cup racing over the last twenty years. The company enjoyed success with Bobby Allison in the 1980s and continue to sponsor and win with Rusty Wallace's #2 car. Here Wallace leads a pack out of the tight turns at Martinsville in the 1997 Goody's 500.*

Beer Wars

As the sponsorship parade hit full swing going into the 1980s, there were some interesting trends in the types of companies that put big dollars into NASCAR teams. The original corporate sponsors took advantage of the tie-in between auto racing and auto products, and oil companies have continued to be among the most prominent sponsors. Fast-food and beverage companies have also been common sponsors, with Hardee's, Burger King, Coca-Cola, and Pepsi all painting their names on the sides of cars.

Another market segment that has been amply represented is the beer industry. By the mid-1980s, at least five breweries were sponsoring stock car teams, in what at times looked like a "battle of the beers." Some remain top team sponsors today, with the Busch division of Anheuser sponsoring the Busch Grand National series and the annual Busch Clash race (to which the pole winners in the previous season are invited).

Carling
1974: #11 and #52 Junior Johnson teams

Busch
1979–1980: #11 Cale Yarborough

Budweiser
1983: #44 Terry Labonte
1984–1986: #11 Darrell Waltrip, #12 Neil Bonnett
1987–1989: #11 Terry Labonte
1990–1991: #11 Geoffery Bodine
1992–1994: #11 Bill Elliott
1995–1996: #25 Ken Schrader
1997: #25 Ricky Craven
1998: #50 Ricky Craven, Wally Dallenbach, and others
1999: #25 Wally Dallenbach and Dale Earnhardt Jr.

Coors
1984–1991: #9 Bill Elliott
1995–1996: #42 Kyle Petty
1997: #40 Robby Gordon and others
1998–1999: #40 Sterling Marlin

Miller
1983–1984: #22 Bobby Allison
1985: #22 Bobby Allison, #77 Greg Sacks
1986–1987: #22 Bobby Allison, #8 Bobby Hillin Jr.
1988: #12 Bobby Allison/Mike Alexander, #8 Bobby Hillin Jr.
1989: #84 Mike Alexander/Dick Trickle, #8 Bobby Hillin Jr.
1990: #27 Rusty Wallace
1991–1999: #2 Rusty Wallace

Old Milwaukee
1983–1985: #27 Tim Richmond

Stroh's
1988–1989: #6 Mark Martin

1979 Championship Standings

Place	Car#	Driver	Car Type	Points
1	43	Richard Petty	Chevy/Olds	4,830
2	88	Darrell Waltrip	Chevy	4,819
3	15	Bobby Allison	Ford	4,633
4	11	Cale Yarborough	Olds	4,604
5	27	Benny Parsons	Chevy/Olds	4,256
6	72	Joe Millikan	Chevy/Olds	4,014
7	2	Dale Earnhardt	Chevy/Olds/Buick	3,749
8	3	Richard Childress	Chevy	3,735
9	90	Ricky Rudd	Mercury	3,642
10	44	Terry Labonte	Chevy/Buick	3,615

race by a mere eleven points—the closest points race in NASCAR history to that point.

While Petty and Waltrip provided excitement at the end of the season, Bobby and Donnie Allison and Cale Yarborough caused the jaws of millions of television viewers to drop at the beginning of the year. The Daytona 500 was to be televised live, in its entirety, for the first time ever, by CBS. The race delivered thrills from the get-go. The Allisons and Yarborough tangled after only thirty laps, putting them all laps down to the leader. Donnie and Cale were able to struggle back to the lead lap, and with twenty laps to go were racing for the win. Then they banged together and both cars spun out into the grass. The audiences at home and at the track were then treated to one of stock car racing's most enduring moments as Cale, Donnie, and Bobby (who had stopped his car to check on his brother) continued the battle in the infield. In the meantime, Petty snuck by and won his sixth Daytona.

If that wasn't enough to make it a spectacular season, 1979 also saw a rookie driver by the name of Dale Earnhardt pick up his first win, after only sixteen starts, in Rod Osterlund's #2. Another young driver, Ricky Rudd, moved into W.C. "Junie" Donlavey Jr.'s #90 when Dick Brooks left that ride. And, for the first time since 1964, there were two Pettys on the track together. Richard's son Kyle finished ninth in his first Winston Cup race, running with grandpap's old number—42—and flying the STP colors.

Bobby Allison returned with Bud Moore and picked up five wins, including a race at Talladega, where a seventeen-car wreck took out most of the front-runners.

There were some big team changes that year as well. Benny Parsons ended his nine-year association with L.G. DeWitt and moved to the M.C. Anderson #27. To everyone's amazement, the superteam of David Pearson and the Wood Brothers split up after the spring Darlington race. The breakup came after a pit miscue (Len Wood said "Whoa!" but Pearson heard "Go!") caused David to pull out without lug nuts on the left side tires. Both tires fell off the car before he made it back on track. Pearson climbed out and walked away. The incident brought matters to a head, but the team hadn't been terribly competitive that year and had had differences about how to remedy the problem. They'd had an amazing run, amassing forty-three wins in their seven years together.

They were the best of buddies but raced each other hard on-track. Neil Bonnett won the 1979 Firecracker 400 at Daytona—his second win since taking over the #21 ride earlier that summer. Despite the appearance of the photo, Dale Earnhardt, in the #2, actually finished third in the race. Earnhardt had already won once that year—a rare feat for a rookie contender.

Great Rivalries in NASCAR

One of the cornerstones of NASCAR's success has been the fans' identification with and loyalty to their favorite drivers. The rivalries between drivers likewise extend to the fans, so that a popular Monday activity is heated comparisons of the drivers' abilities and performances (not to mention parentage, fondness for drink, and so on).

Petty Versus Allison

There have been some pretty intense rivalries between drivers in the history of the Winston Cup, but none more vivid than that between Richard Petty and Bobby Allison. The contrast between their driving styles and the fact that they often found themselves in close competition for a win led to some colorful incidents.

In 1967, Allison linked up with two competitive teams, the #6 Cotton Owens Dodge, then the Holman-Moody #11 Ford, and was racing for wins (he got six) and a top spot in the points. Petty had a banner year, winning twenty-seven races and taking the championship. Along the way, he and Allison earned several of their wins by pushing the other out of the way. The short tracks were their battleground, with Petty wedging past Allison to take a win at Columbia, South Carolina. Weeks later at Weaverville, North Carolina, another half-mile (0.8km) track, Allison and Petty swapped the lead back and forth throughout the race. Near the end, a pass by Petty sent Allison spinning to the wall. Allison caught up and returned the favor, going on for the win. The #11 and #43 pit stalls emptied quickly after the race as the crews rushed together to "discuss" the action. "Things like that happen on short tracks when you have two cars that are equal and two drivers who want to win badly," explained Allison.

The two renewed their rivalry in 1972, again on the short tracks. As in 1967, they found themselves competing week after week, and by the time they reached Richmond to start the autumn short-track segment, they had had about enough of each other. Though Petty and Allison denied that they had a feud going, their actions on the track said otherwise.

Petty got the Richmond win after his car was propelled up onto the steel guardrail in a tangle with Allison. Petty took the Martinsville race as well, though he almost went a lap down to Allison after a pit stop. NASCAR had given Petty the "move over" flag to let Allison by, but he ignored it, made up his lap, and got the win. Allison was actually fined after the race for ignoring a black flag given him when his gas cap was knocked loose in the rubbing with Petty. But the real fireworks—both on and off the track—came the following week at North Wilkesboro. Allison and Petty spent the last forty laps of the race in constant contact, swapping the lead ten times. The fans were ecstatic—this was the kind of hard, close racing that filled stands and made NASCAR stand out among motorsports. With only three laps left, Petty and Allison sent each other into the wall twice, with Petty getting the better of the last contact and taking the win.

After the Wilkesboro race, both drivers were willing to talk feud. After blowing off steam, though, they attributed their actions, as they had in 1967, to the nature of short-track racing and assured NASCAR that the close contact would not continue at the higher speeds of the superspeedways. Whether by intention or coincidence, they were right, and the on-track duels ended when they moved on to Charlotte.

Waltrip and Yarborough

Darrell Waltrip was a new breed of racer, who combined razor-sharp driving skills with a razor-sharp wit. Darrell understood the value of the media—how to play them and how to play to them. There was no doubt about his driving ability, but his competitors sometimes took his outspoken manner for arrogance and egotism. Cale Yarborough, for one, didn't always appreciate Waltrip's ready quips, and in 1977 the two engaged in a rivalry of words.

It started at the Southern 500. Waltrip and Yarborough were fighting for the lead in heavy traffic with about one hundred laps to go. Charging into turn three side by side, neither would back off as they ran up on lapped cars. The two were able to drive away from the resulting wreck, which damaged the cars of D.K. Ulrich, Janet Guthrie, and Terry Blivins. After the race, Ulrich asked Yarborough why he put him in the wall.

"Jaws hit you," Yarborough replied.

"Who?" asked Ulrich.

"You know, Waltrip. Jaws. Always talking."

Yarborough later explained that he was really just kidding, but Darrell wasted no time coming back with a retort. After winning the five-hundred-lap race at Martinsville, Cale was exhausted and complained that five hundred laps was too many. The following week in the winner's circle at North Wilkesboro, Waltrip proposed the "Cale Scale," a way of rating the difficulty of races based on how Yarborough felt afterward. "I guess Cale is getting too old," drawled Jaws.

Yarborough had the last laugh that year, though: he won his second championship by more than five hundred points over Waltrip, who wound up in fourth place. As Jaws, Waltrip would also find himself in the role of bad guy to many Winston Cup fans for years to come. At one point during driver introductions

in 1982, irritated at repeatedly being booed, the feisty Waltrip invited the detractors in the crowd to meet him in the Big K parking lot to settle their differences.

Earnhardt and...Everyone Else

Dale Earnhardt's take-no-prisoners style of driving earned him the enmity of several competitors over the years. Even so, their recognition of his tremendous talent and his unpretentious personality turned many of those rivals into friends.

Earnhardt's reputation for rough driving and the nickname "Ironhead" emerged in the mid-1980s. Earnhardt snatched a pair of victories from rising star Tim Richmond in 1985 by applying his bumper to the back of Richmond's car near the end of the races. But Richmond was a tough racer in the same mold as Earnhardt; the two were friends and respected each other's abilities. Richmond shrugged off the incident: "I'm not mad; it was good hard racing."

Earnhardt, who had grown up watching the aggressive driving tactics of his father (nicknamed "Ironheart") and of contemporaries like Curtis Turner, came under fire for applying those tactics in 1986. After punting Darrell Waltrip out of the lead at Richmond, thereby causing a multicar accident, Earnhardt was put on probation for a year for reckless driving. By 1987, Earnhardt had become something of a universal excuse for not winning a race. Sterling Marlin, Alan Kulwicki, Geoff (now Geoffrey) Bodine, and Harry Gant all took issue with his style.

In the 1990s, Earnhardt found himself in a (usually) friendly rivalry with Rusty Wallace. Earnhardt and Wallace were the two

For most of the 1998 season, Jeff Gordon and Mark Martin (seen here battling for the lead at Michigan International Speedway at the Pepsi 400 in August) were in first and second place, respectively, in the points standings. No matter how well Martin did, though, it seemed as if Gordon would do just a bit better. The frustration in Martin's camp finally led to an accusation late in the season that Gordon's team was using illegal tire additives (that is, cheating); after an examination by the NASCAR sanctioning board, however, Gordon was exonerated. Thus are some rivalries born.

masters of the short tracks early in the decade and often found themselves trading paint for the win. Though close friends, they have had their tense moments. Contact with Earnhardt's car sent Wallace's Ford tumbling through the air at Talladega in 1993 as they scrambled for position in a one-lap restart. Though Wallace didn't place blame, he reminded Earnhardt of the incident a couple of years later after a bump from the #3 put him in the wall at Bristol. "I haven't forgotten Talladega!" shouted Rusty after the race, accompanying his words with a thrown water bottle.

Earnhardt took a page from Waltrip's playbook in trying to find a way to deal with the amazing success of heir-apparent Jeff Gordon. Poking fun at Gordon's youth and squeaky-clean image, Earnhardt dubbed him "Wonder Boy" and, inevitably, "Flash" Gordon. After winning the second running of the Brickyard 400 (Gordon had won the first), Earnhardt quipped that he was the first "man" to win the race. Gordon's reply was to win the championship.

Chapter Three

The Changing of the Guard: 1980 to 1984

Each era of NASCAR has had its great figures, superstars who defined the time and the sport. As one generation of drivers neared the end of their careers, there was always another crop of fresh-faced kids eager to emulate their heroes. As Lee Petty, Curtis Turner, and Buck Baker had stepped aside, Richard Petty, Cale Yarborough, and Buddy Baker were standing in the wings, itching to take the reins.

By 1980, Petty, Pearson, and Yarborough were in their third or fourth decades with NASCAR. When they first broke into the Grand National ranks there were at most three or four really competitive teams running in most races. If you hooked up with a quality team, you had a good chance of winning on a regular basis. By the late 1970s, with more corporate sponsorship money available, there were more teams running at the top level, which meant that the dominant drivers of the 1960s and early 1970s were finding it harder to build a winning streak. The likelihood of anyone repeating Richard Petty's 1967 feat of winning twenty-seven races in a season was virtually nil, and even his thirteen wins of 1975 would be tough to match.

Though Richard Petty ended the decade on a high note with his seventh championship, the #43 team was unable to extend that success into the next decade. Petty would win only ten more races up to his last, in 1984. The Petty juggernaut was slowed by a combination of things. Richard, still recovering from his illness, suffered serious injuries in two accidents in 1980 that affected his ability to race full-bore. There were also significant changes in car models, as NASCAR downsized in 1981. Petty and crew struggled with the Buick Regal (following an abortive reunion attempt with Chrysler in the form of the Dodge Mirada), then with Pontiacs. To add to his difficulties, one of Petty's last wins (number 198) was tainted by allegations of cheating. In the postrace inspection, NASCAR found that the engine was considerably larger than the maximum allowed size. Petty was heavily fined—both money and championship points—though he was allowed to retain the win.

Changes in the Richard Petty Enterprises (RPE) team played a big role as well. Petty's longtime friend and crew chief Dale Inman left the team in 1981 to join Rod Osterlund. RPE had extended its stable to two cars in 1979 to accommodate Kyle Petty's entry into racing and had trouble adjusting to the change. After a winless 1983 season, Richard announced that he would leave RPE, taking the #43 STP colors to Mike Curb's team for 1984. Kyle's operation stayed with RPE. Though Richard would soon return when Kyle moved on to other teams, the Petty magic was gone.

David Pearson's departure from the #21 team gave other teams a chance to win on the superspeedways. Pearson continued driving with other teams and with his own car until 1986, but never repeated his earlier successes. In 1980, he won just one race, the last victory of his amazing career.

In 1980, Cale Yarborough was still going strong with Junior Johnson's team, but he soon decided he'd had enough of the pressures of pursuing the championship full-time. In a surprise move, Cale left the #11 team after 1980 and cut back to a part-time schedule. Top drivers Benny Parsons and Buddy Baker also found themselves running partial schedules through most of the 1980s. Parsons continued full-time with M.C. Anderson, then moved to Bud Moore's team in 1981. Starting in 1982, Parsons ran with Johnny Hayes in the Skoal #55 and briefly in Rick Hendrick's #35 until his crossover from the cockpit to the broadcast booth in 1989. Buddy Baker spent several seasons with the Ranier team, then the Wood Brothers, before forming his own team with Danny Schiff in 1985.

The Youngbloods
As the veterans cut back or struggled to regain top form, a new group of talented drivers was coming up to fill in the gaps. Darrell Waltrip, who had been on the scene since 1972, bridged the generations. By 1980, Darrell was successful and on the verge of taking over the top spot in the series.

Neil Bonnett, from Hueytown, Alabama—also the hometown of "Alabama Gang" leaders Bobby and Donnie Allison—had graduated from working in Bobby Allison's shop to driving by subbing for Bobby in 1976. The popular driver soon landed solid, if temporary, rides with the K&K and Jim Stacy teams, and by 1979 he had been called by the Wood Brothers team to replace Pearson in the legendary #21.

The rookie class of 1979 was an amazing one. Its members—Dale Earnhardt, Harry Gant, Terry Labonte, and Joe Millikan—included future champions, crowd favorites, and a man who would be "King."

Dale Earnhardt was a second-generation racer who had earned a ride with Rod Osterlund for the 1979 season by demonstrating his prowess in a one-race deal the previous year. Osterlund was fielding a car for Willy T. Ribbs for the World 600, but when Ribbs failed to show up for any of his practice sessions, Earnhardt was given the ride. Earnhardt's innate talent and fierce determination brought him his first

Winston Cup championship in 1980, his sophomore year. Six more championships would follow over the years, tying "King" Richard's record, a feat assumed to be impossible in the modern era (though it looks as if Jeff Gordon may equal, and even surpass, it one day).

Sportsman series star Harry Gant was another candidate for Rookie of the Year in 1979. Gant had raced sporadically in Winston Cup competition since 1973, but had concentrated on a successful Sportsman career (and his "real" job, building houses). At thirty-nine, Gant, deciding to give WC his full-time attention, drove Kenny Childer's #12 and Jack Beebe's #47 cars. One of the best-liked drivers of all time, among both fans and competitors, Gant partnered with Hollywood producer Hal Needham and actor Burt Reynolds in 1981, taking on the enduring persona of the "Skoal Bandit," named for the Skoal brand of sponsor U.S. Tobacco. Gant's association with Needham landed him in the movies as well as in a premier ride; Gant appeared in *Stroker Ace* (1983) and *Days of Thunder* (1990).

Terry Labonte had worked as a crewmember on Billy Hagan's #92 team for most of 1978, but replaced driver Skip Manning behind the wheel near the end of the year. When the Texas oil baron's team changed to #44 in 1979, Labonte was the pilot. Terry's talent was obvious—the team had twelve top-ten finishes and came up tenth in the points in its first season. Labonte and Hagan went on to win the 1984 championship and stayed together until 1994. Labonte scored his second championship in 1996, with Rick Hendrick's #5 team.

Though it was a tight rookie race in 1979 and Joe Millikan finished highest in the points standings among the candidates, Earnhardt won the Rookie of the Year honors.

Other stars of the new generation included Ricky Rudd and Tim Richmond. Rudd, who made his first Winston Cup appearance in 1975, started earning top-fives in his father's #22 car in 1977, and would replace Darrell Waltrip in the DiGard ride in 1981. Rudd started a long streak of winning seasons in 1983, with Richard Childress and the #3.

Tim Richmond was a racer cut from a different cloth. Not only did he possess the skills and competitiveness to bang bumpers with the sport's best and come out on top, but he also had the looks and charisma of a Hollywood star. Richmond came to NASCAR from Indy racing in 1980, and by 1983 was in Raymond Beadle's new "Blue Max" #27 car, winning races.

One other name should be mentioned here. A quiet young redhead from Georgia had made a handful of starts each year since 1976 in his family-owned #9. Partnering with Detroit industrialist Harry Melling, Bill Elliott would hit the big time, in a big way, in the 1980s.

PAGE 76: *"Handsome Harry" Gant was one of the most popular of all Winston Cup drivers. Here, he poses with his signature Skoal Bandit car in 1981, his first year with that ride.* PAGE 77: *A stack of wheel rims at Martinsville in 1988. Goodyear mounts hundreds of tires for each Winston Cup race. In 1988, for the first time in decades, Goodyear was joined by another tire provider for the series. Unfortunately, competition among tire manufacturers sometimes compromises the safety of the drivers and cars.* RIGHT: *Cale Yarborough (left) and Buddy Baker swap stories in the garage in 1981.* BELOW: *Earnhardt cuts to the inside of Yarborough (#27) in the 1981 Southern 500 at Darlington. Terry Labonte, still carrying Stacy sponsorship on the Billy Hagan #44 car, is in the chase.*

NASCAR Downsizes

The repercussions of the 1973 oil embargo were long-term and widespread. With the cost of oil doubling overnight, the Detroit auto manufacturers began downsizing their cars to more fuel-efficient and economical models. By the 1980s, the land yachts of the 1960s and 1970s had been replaced by smaller and lighter vehicles.

NASCAR understood that it would eventually have to follow suit. There was a three-year eligibility rule on car models, but, recalling the difficulties and expenses involved in model changes in the past, NASCAR relaxed the rules in 1977. When the 1974 models were phased out in 1978, the organization—realizing that neither it nor the teams were ready to go to smaller makes—approved the larger models for another cycle. By 1981, it was time to change. New models were identified well in advance to give teams sufficient time to change over. The models would be, by manufacturer: GM (Buick Regal, Chevy Monte Carlo or Malibu, Olds Cutlass Supreme, Pontiac LeMans or Grand Prix), Ford (Ford Thunderbird, Mercury Cougar or Monarch), and Chrysler (Chrysler LeBaron, Dodge Mirada).

Most GM teams went with the Monte Carlo, Regal, or Grand Prix. Almost all Ford teams used the T-Bird. Early tests yielded predictable results—the smaller 110-inch

Young gun Tim Richmond joined the Winston Cup ranks as a rookie in 1981. Richmond went to a full schedule for the 1981 season in a D.K. Ulrich Buick. 1981 was Darrell Waltrip's year, though, and everyone else was running for second on back. Richmond was no exception, and his Uno car ended up seventeenth here in the Richmond 400.

(2.8m) wheelbase cars (down from 115 inches [2.9m]) were as fast as the old cars but much less stable. To compensate, NASCAR increased spoiler sizes from 216 to 250 square inches (1.4m²–1.6m²), then again to 276 square inches (1.8m²) before the Daytona 500.

The Ranier-Allison team took a different tack. Allison took the pole at Daytona with a qualifying speed of nearly 2 mph (3.2kph) faster than the average in the only Pontiac LeMans in the field. The LeMans showed such promise in the early races that NASCAR issued another rules change in March, tying spoiler sizes to car models. As expected, the LeMans was penalized. Rather than suffer the disadvantage, the Ranier team switched to Buicks, and the LeMans was off the scene as quickly as it had arrived.

Though two Chrysler models were listed, tests by the RPE team showed them to be significantly slower than the other makes, and that was the end of the line for Chrysler in NASCAR.

Cable TV Although ABC and CBS had increased their coverage of NASCAR racing, relatively few of a season's races were televised, usually only the ones on the major speedways.

In 1981, NASCAR found a new outlet for promotion. Entertainment Sports Programming Network (ESPN) announced that it was interested in broadcasting Winston Cup races. The network proposed broadcasting six races, live and uncut, in 1982.

As cable increased in popularity, more channels came on the air looking for new programming. Each track was free to make its own deal with networks, and soon The Nashville Network (TNN) and the Turner Broadcasting System (TBS) added NASCAR coverage as well. By 1990, all Winston Cup and Grand National events could be seen on television.

The Big Money Men For most of the teams on the circuit, especially the so-called "independents," racing was a way of life but also very much a business. They needed all the money they earned with wins and top finishes to pay their bills or to invest in their cars. By the 1980s, NASCAR was attracting attention and interest from a wide cross-section of American society and the business community. As more teams were formed with a greater diversity of sponsorships, the sport also began to benefit from investment by "hobbyists"—wealthy businessmen who saw success in Winston Cup not as a business

opportunity but as a personal goal. Several of these ambitious industrialists stood out both for their level of investment in the sport and, unfortunately, for the fate of their operations.

Jim (J.D.) Stacy was a Kentucky coal-mine investor who first got into racing in 1977. He put his own name on the quarterpanel of a #5 Dodge and hired driver Neil Bonnett and ace mechanic Harry Hyde. Not surprisingly with that kind of talent, the team won two races in their first year. The next year—1978—was a different story, though. After Hyde sued Stacy partway through the season over nonpayment for shop space, equipment, and other debts, the shop ended up closing. The team was in a shambles, but Stacy leased cars from Rod Osterlund for Bonnett to finish the season. Stacy had also run the #6 car with Ferrell Harris as driver; Harris also brought suit against Stacy over repayment of a loan.

Stacy lay low from 1978 to 1980, but was back in business in 1981. To make his comeback he again turned to Rod Osterlund. The Californian had a championship team but was in need of quick cash so he sold the team to Stacy in June 1981. Within a couple of months, most of the crew had either left or been released, while ace driver Dale Earnhardt quit to drive for Richard Childress, taking the Wrangler sponsorship with him. Joe Ruttman finished the season in the blue and yellow J.D. Stacy #2 Buick.

In 1982, Stacy took the "more is better" approach and ran two teams from his shops (Ruttman in #2 and first Jim Sauter, then Robin McCall, in #5). He also sponsored five

The Stavola brothers ran a multicar operation in the late 1980s. Bobby Allison's #12 was retired after his last race in 1988 and Dick Trickle picked up the ride in #84. Like Johnson's two-car team in the early 1980s (and unlike any multicar teams since), both cars sported the same sponsor, Miller High Life.

other teams (Marcis' #71, Beebe's #47, Ranier's #28, Hagan's #44, and Donlavey's #90). Tim Richmond took over for Ruttman in April and brought the team two wins, but financial problems were cropping up again. Stacy pulled sponsorship from the #71 and #44 for questionable reasons, and Ranier pulled his name from the #28 when the sponsorship checks stopped coming. Richmond, leery of the team's instability, left at the end of the year. By 1983, Stacy's empire had shrunk to one team, which folded the next year.

M.C. Anderson, owner of a successful Georgia construction company, had been in NASCAR since 1976, running the #27 team with Sam Sommers, Buddy Baker, and Benny Parsons. In 1981, Anderson landed Cale Yarborough when Cale left Junior Johnson's operation. They had good sponsorship from Valvoline, and Anderson spent big bucks to bring in quality team members. Yarborough, however, had signed on with the understanding that he would run only a limited schedule. Anderson pressured him to run the full circuit for a try at the championship in 1983, reputedly offering him $1 million to do so. After Yarborough refused, Anderson, disappointed and evidently feeling that no other available driver could fill Cale's shoes, decided to close down the team.

Californian Warren Hodgdon purchased part ownership of several Winston Cup tracks—Bristol, North Wilkesboro, Richmond, and Nashville—in 1981 and put his name on the side of the Wood Brothers #21 car. In 1983, Wood Brothers driver Neil Bonnett moved on to the Rahmoc #75 team, with Hodgdon as sponsor and part owner. Hodgdon took another big step in 1984, buying into Junior Johnson's #11 team and funding a second Johnson team, the #12, again with Neil Bonnett as driver. Dave Marcis took over in the Hodgdon-Rahmoc #75 car.

By 1985, it was all over, and Hodgdon was gone from the scene as rapidly as he had arrived. Facing more than $50 million in suits as a result of improprieties by an employee in his engineering company, Hodgdon filed for bankruptcy in January 1985. Johnson and Rahmoc assumed full control of their teams, and Warren Hodgdon was out of racing.

A third-generation Petty joined Petty Enterprises in 1979. In 1983 Kyle switched from #42 to #7 for his 7-Eleven sponsorship. To try and relieve the strain of the two-car operation, Kyle's team moved to a separate facility at the back of the Petty shops. It didn't help much, though, and this was the last two-car year until PE2 was formed for Kyle in 1997.

Rookie of the Year

A yearly influx of new talent has kept NASCAR racing alive and growing over the decades. Each year, NASCAR sponsors a Rookie of the Year award to recognize the best of the new arrivals. To qualify for the award, a driver must race in more than five points events during the year. To determine the winner, the average finishes of all competitors are compared, with the best and worst finish for each discarded to reduce the effects of chance. Just the same, the selection isn't strictly objective—a panel reviews the records, takes into account any special circumstances or remarkable performances, and decides who is most deserving of the award.

The Rookie of the Year program was started in 1958. It was won that year by Lloyd "Shorty" Rollins, who had had an upset victory in a 50-miler (80km) at State Line Speedway in New York. Rollins is on a short list of drivers who won races in their rookie year: Earl Ross got his only victory in 1974 as a rookie; Dale Earnhardt had one win in 1979, which helped him beat Joe Millikan, Terry Labonte, and Harry Gant in the rookie race; and Davey Allison holds the record, with two victories in 1987 (his first season), in Harry Ranier's #28 car. Tony Stewart is the only rookie since then to win a race (he won three in 1999).

Many of the sport's champions took the rookie honors in their time. Richard Petty, David Pearson, Earnhardt, Rusty Wallace, Alan Kulwicki, and Jeff Gordon were all top rookies. Notable by their absence are Darrell Waltrip, who lost the

TOP: *Few drivers have had as successful a rookie year as Dale Earnhardt, who placed seventh in the points race despite missing several races due to a broken collarbone. The rookie is seen here in a Buick during a race on February 18, 1979.*
LEFT: *Between mechanical problems and crashes, Rob Moroso was able to log only one top-ten finish in his rookie year in 1990. The talented driver wouldn't have the chance to improve on his record—on his way home from dinner following the fall North Wilkesboro race, he lost control of his car and was killed in a collision.*

1973 battle to Lennie Pond; Bobby Allison; Cale Yarborough; and Bill Elliott, who ran short schedules in their rookie years.

Dick Trickle, who won in 1989 at forty-seven years old, was the oldest Rookie of the Year. Trickle had dominated regional short tracks before turning his attention to Winston Cup, and he is believed to have won more stock car races—more than a thousand—than any other NASCAR driver.

The Rookie of the Year award was voted posthumously in 1990 to Rob Moroso. Moroso, who had had a tough first year, but showed real talent and promise as a driver, was tragically killed in an auto accident at the end of September 1990.

Most rookies start their careers with low-budget rides. In 1998 Kenny Irwin stepped into every Winston Cup hopeful's dream—a ride with a top team—when Robert Yates named him to replace Ernie Irvan in the potent Texaco #28 car.

1980: A New Gunslinger

The year 1980 belonged to Dale Earnhardt. Earnhardt and the Osterlund #2 team had run well in 1979, finishing with a top-ten in the points standings and the Rookie of the Year award. Earnhardt finished second in the 1980 season opener at Riverside behind Waltrip, then took the points lead at Daytona. The team went on to win at Atlanta, Charlotte, and three of the short-track races. At times throughout the year their lead was challenged by several veteran teams—Allison, Petty, and Yarborough all came close. The team's success was also threatened when it lost crew chief Jake Elder, who was replaced by thirty-year-old Doug Richert.

Earnhardt's duel with Cale Yarborough came down to the last race of the season. When Earnhardt went down a lap early on, it looked like Cale would win his fourth title. The #2 fought back, though, and regained the lead lap on a caution. Cale finished third, and Earnhardt fifth, his points lead whittled to nineteen, but still enough for the sophomore team to win the championship. Osterlund brought on Wrangler Jeans sponsorship late in the year and Dale "One Tough Customer" Earnhardt and crew looked good for a repeat in 1981.

Darrell Waltrip's troubles at DiGard resurfaced in 1980. Darrell was unhappy with the Gardners' attempt to fund a second car at Daytona (unsuccessfully, it turned out, as driver Don Whittington failed to qualify), and with mechanical demons that plagued the team throughout the season. At one point, Waltrip had to bum a ride from Joel Halpern to make the field at Michigan, when two DiGard cars blew engines during qualifying. The shop's revolving door was turning again, too: crew chief Buddy Parrott was fired twice, and "Suitcase" Jake Elder returned. By October, Waltrip was once more jockeying to get out of his contract with the team and making no bones about it with the press. By the end of the year, owner Bill Gardner, who apparently had had enough of Waltrip's antics, allowed him to buy out of the deal. No figures were released, but Darrell's freedom is said to have cost him nearly half a million dollars.

Besides winning five races, the team accomplished one of the most amazing feats in the Winston Cup garage. In 1980, the last year that NASCAR would allow teams to change blown engines during a race, the DiGard team swapped Darrell's smoking engine at Martinsville in a record eleven minutes, twenty-six seconds. Try getting that kind of service at your local garage.

An unexpected announcement in the fall of 1980 opened up the top ride on the circuit just as Waltrip, finally free of the #88 team, was looking for a new ride for 1981. After eight years and three championships, Cale Yarborough let out that 1980 would be his last year with Junior Johnson. Yarborough wanted to cut back his schedule to spend more time with his family and would run a limited number of races with M.C. Anderson.

With the #11 ride open, Waltrip moved to Johnson's team. Ricky Rudd signed on at DiGard in his place (he only stayed one year), leaving the #90 car open for Jody Ridley. Buddy Baker won two races with the Ranier team in 1980—including his first Daytona 500. Neil Bonnett picked up two more wins with the Wood Brothers, and Terry Labonte got his first career win in the prestigious Southern 500, slipping past the leaders as they wrecked with twenty-one laps to go. In his last year with them, Benny Parsons led the M.C. Anderson team to a third-place finish in the points and three wins.

Richard Petty had a tough season. He sustained a broken neck in an end-over-end accident at Pocono that hampered him for the rest of the year. His son Kyle, in the second RPE car, ran fifteen races, with six top-ten finishes. A young driver by the name of Rusty Wallace made an impression in his first Winston Cup start, finishing second in a Roger Penske Chevy at Atlanta.

Dale Earnhardt

Dale Earnhardt has earned many nicknames throughout his career—including "One Tough Customer," "Ironhead," "The Intimidator," and "The Man in Black"—but perhaps the one that sums things up best is "Seven-Time Champion." Earnhardt is the driver most often compared to Richard Petty as a "king" of stock car racing.

Earnhardt started his racing education at his father's knee. Ralph Earnhardt was a tough, smart racer, and Dale paid close attention to his lessons as he grew up. Earnhardt first broke into Winston Cup racing in 1975 in Ed Negre's #8 Dodge. In 1978, Dale got a break, picking up a ride at Charlotte when the intended driver (Willy T. Ribbs) didn't show for the race.

Later that year, Earnhardt hooked up with Rod Osterlund for several successful seasons: he was Rookie of the Year in 1979 and, in his sophomore year, Winston Cup champion. In 1981, after Osterlund sold the team to J.D. Stacy, Earnhardt left, picking up the remainder of the season with Richard Childress, who had recently turned from driver to owner, in the latter's #3. Childress recognized Earnhardt's talent, going so far as to acknowledge that his young team didn't have the equipment Earnhardt deserved.

Dale became "One Tough Customer" in 1982, driving Bud Moore's #15 Fords. He also began to acquire a reputation as a tough customer on the track—one who wouldn't hesitate to use his front bumper to get by.

At the end of 1983, Chevy lured Earnhardt away from Moore, and he rejoined Richard Childress, taking the Wrangler colors with him. Earnhardt has been with Childress since then, and the partnership has certainly been one of the most successful in Winston Cup history, yielding championships in 1986, 1987, 1990, 1991, 1993, and 1994 and more than fifty wins, including victories on superspeedways, short tracks, and a road course. Until 1998, the only major milestone that had eluded Earnhardt was a Daytona 500 win (and the ways in which he missed the win over the years, frequently on the last lap, have become legend).

With seven championships, Earnhardt has tied Richard Petty's record, and with a number of solid years of racing left, he has as good a chance as anyone to break it.

1980 Championship Standings

Place	Car#	Driver	Car Type	Points
1	2	Dale Earnhardt	Chevy	4,681
2	11	Cale Yarborough	Chevy	4,642
3	27	Benny Parsons	Chevy	4,278
4	43	Richard Petty	Chevy	4,255
5	88	Darrell Waltrip	Chevy	4,239
6	15	Bobby Allison	Ford	4,019
7	90	Jody Ridley	Ford	3,972
8	44	Terry Labonte	Chevy	3,766
9	71	Dave Marcis	Chevy	3,745
10	3	Richard Childress	Chevy	3,742

A face every racing fan knows. Dale Earnhardt is a canny businessman as well as racer, and was among the first to insist on full control over merchandising of his name and image. As a result of that, and his unparalleled popularity, Dale Earnhardt, Inc. earns the champion more each year than his racing winnings do.

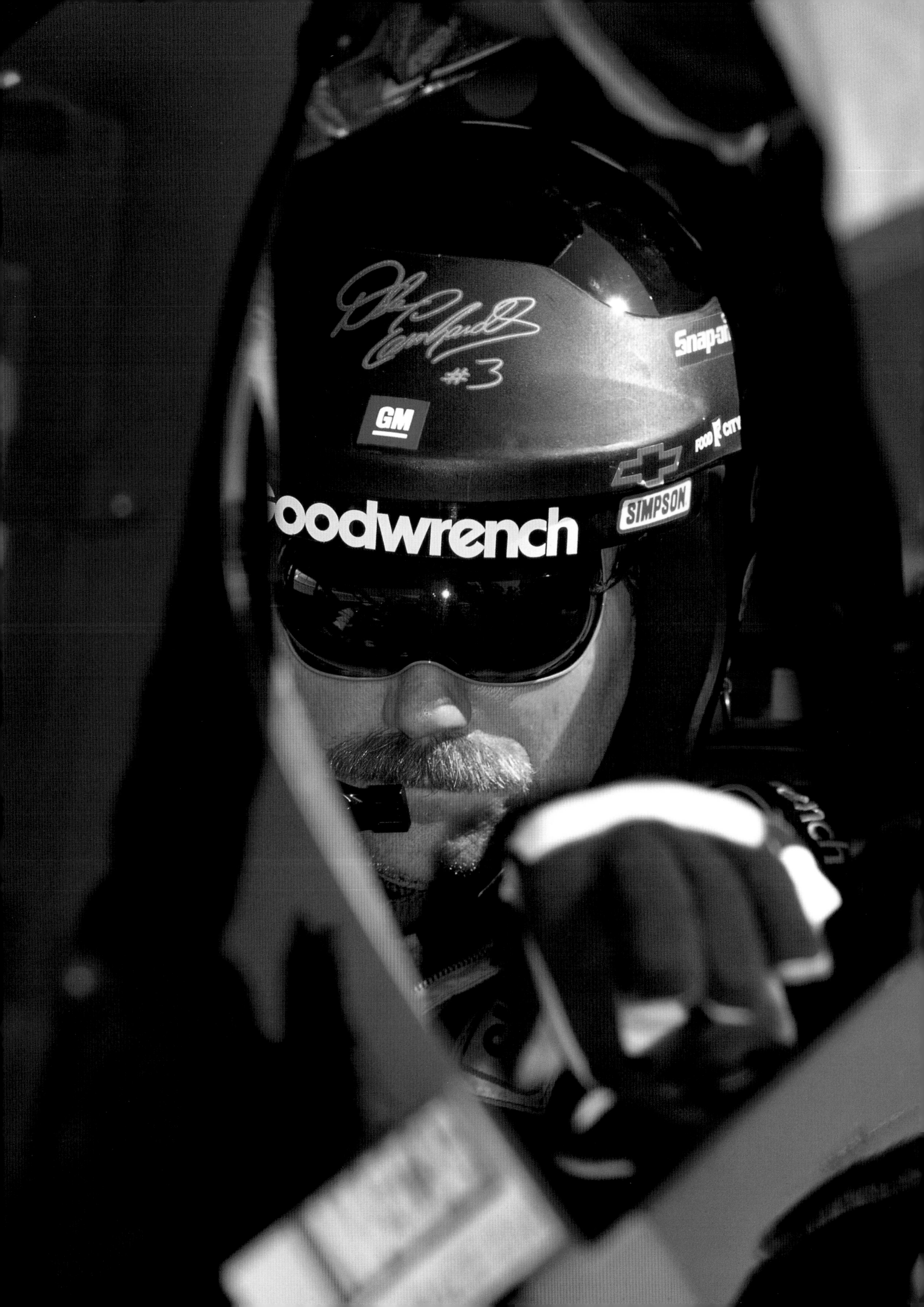
#3
GM
SIMPSON

Harry Gant and the Skoal Bandit team formed a longstanding relationship in 1981. Among his many nicknames, Gant was known as "Bridesmaid Harry" for the string of ten second-place finishes he endured before breaking through with a win in 1982 at Martinsville. It would be the first of eighteen in his successful career.

1981: *Waltrip Proves His Mettle and the "Bandit" Rides into Town*

The 1981 season was dominated by changes in car models as NASCAR downsized. Although Chevy, Buick, Olds, Pontiac, and Ford were represented (with a leftover Dodge or two), Buick was the predominant model, winning twenty-two races.

Twelve of those twenty-two wins were bagged by one team. Waltrip and Junior Johnson hit the track running in 1981, starting off the season with wins at Richmond, Rockingham, Bristol, and Darlington. The team then hit a midseason slump, leaving them several hundred points behind Bobby Allison in June. Waltrip went into high gear then and won half of the remaining races (including an impressive four in a row) to pull ahead of Allison and take his first championship.

Waltrip's chief competition came from Bobby Allison. The #28 Ranier team started out the season in a Pontiac LeMans, the only team to do so. Even after rules changes required them to abandon the model (they switched to

The Skoal Bandit

One of the most popular figures in racing, Harry Gant's Skoal Bandit was born in 1981, when Gant teamed up with Hollywood celebrities Hal Needham and Burt Reynolds and their sponsor, U.S. Tobacco. The pair had first tapped Stan Barrett as their driver, but Gant soon took over the reins. After Gant retired in 1994, Robert Pressley stepped into the ride. He was later replaced by Ken Schrader.

1981 Championship Standings

Place	Car#	Driver	Car Type	Points
1	11	Darrell Waltrip	Buick	4,880
2	28	Bobby Allison	Buick	4,827
3	33	Harry Gant	Pontiac	4,210
4	44	Terry Labonte	Buick	4,052
5	90	Jody Ridley	Ford	4,002
6	88	Ricky Rudd	Buick	3,988
7	3	Dale Earnhardt	Pontiac	3,975
8	43	Richard Petty	Buick	3,880
9	71	Dave Marcis	Buick	3,507
10	15	Benny Parsons	Ford	3,449

Darrell Waltrip

Ol' "D.W.," who celebrated his twenty-fifth anniversary in stock car competition in 1997, is today's elder statesman of Winston Cup racing. In his younger days, however, Waltrip was considered anything but a diplomat. Nicknamed "Jaws" for his aggressive and outspoken approach, D.W. set out early to show that he was just as good, or better, than the beloved old guard of the day.

Waltrip certainly proved his point: in his quarter-century career, Darrell has earned eighty-four wins so far, tying him with Bobby Allison for third in career wins. Teamed up with Junior Johnson, Waltrip also won three championships, in 1981, 1982, and 1985.

Waltrip has a reputation as a thinking driver, as well as a hard-charger—his last two wins, for example, came through careful pit strategy. In a championship battle, Waltrip proved to be as proficient at the psychology of racing as at on-track maneuvers, psyching Bill Elliott out of the 1985 championship as much as outracing him. Darrell's affable manner and on-screen charisma have made him a perennial fan favorite.

In 1997, the team sported color schemes from each of Darrell's past rides, as well as a special chrome "Quicksilver" car. In 1998, Waltrip raced his own #17 team, and also subbed for Steve Park in the #1, earning a top-five finish and taking over the #35 ride. In 1999 D.W. hooked up with a new Travis Carter team.

Top: *Waltrip won the coveted Daytona 500 running on fumes in 1989—he stretched his last run so far that he ran out of gas on the way to victory lane.* Above: *Johnson's #11 team went through several changes for the 1983 season, switching from Buicks to Chevys and replacing the Mountain Dew colors with Pepsi. The lineup was basically the same, though, with D.W. driving and Jeff Hammond returning as crew chief.*

Kyle Petty (seen here on July 9, 1982) drove for two teams through much of the 1982 season—not consecutively but alternately. Testing the waters on moving out of the family-owned Petty Enterprises, he drove a handful of races for Hoss Ellington, extending STP sponsorship to that ride, as well as competing in the #42 car. Kyle returned to Petty full-time the following year.

Buicks), the team was strong. They picked up five wins and held the lead in points through the first half of the year, ultimately yielding to Waltrip's blitzkrieg with only a handful of races left.

Dale Earnhardt, with new sponsorship from Wrangler, hoped for a reprise of his extraordinary 1980 season. Not only did the team not repeat that performance; it didn't even survive the year. After denying any intention of doing so, Rod Osterlund sold the team in June—to Jim Stacy, under whose stewardship it self-destructed within a couple of months. Earnhardt went on to drive for Richard Childress, who had driven his own cars in NASCAR for twelve years without much success. With the opportunity to employ a talent like Earnhardt, Childress quickly stepped out of the car. The team managed a handful of top-tens, and Earnhardt finished seventh in the points standings.

Several new teams were formed in 1981. One that would be a front-runner for years to come was put together by Hollywood personalities Hal Needham and Burt Reynolds. They had selected Stan Barrett to drive their #22 Skoal Bandit car, but after seeing Harry Gant's second-

place run at Atlanta asked him on as a second-team driver. Gant's #33 quickly became a weekly threat and crowd favorite. Barrett left the team before midseason. Furniture manufacturer Cliff Stewart also started a new team (the #5) with Morgan Shepherd, then Joe Millikan, as driver.

Jody Ridley won his first race and brought Junie Donlavey his first and only Winston Cup victory at Dover in May. It was a strange win, and Bobby Allison contested it. NASCAR officials admitted that they had experienced "scoring difficulties" during the race, and there was some doubt about whether Ridley was in the same lap as Allison. The win was upheld, though, and after thirty-one years as a car owner, Donlavey was in the winners' circle.

Mark Martin, an ASA (American Speed Assocation) hotshot from the Midwest, ran his own team in Winston Cup competition in 1981. He qualified on the pole in his third race, at Nashville, and finished eleventh.

Richard Petty showed a flash of the old style at the beginning of the year, winning his seventh Daytona 500. Veteran Donnie Allison suffered serious injuries in a wreck at Charlotte in May that ended his season. Though Allison would continue racing through 1988, he never resumed a full-time schedule and was unable to add to his ten career Winston Cup wins.

1982: Waltrip Edges Allison— Again

Darrell Waltrip became the comeback king with his championship defense in 1982. Waltrip and Bobby Allison spent much of the season trading the top spot in the points standings. Allison had left the Ranier ride at the end of 1981 and signed on with DiGard, Waltrip's old team. DiGard was as strong with Allison as it had been with Darrell, and with only seven races left in the season had what seemed like a comfortable 147-point lead. Waltrip then put together another late-season surge to take over at the top with just three races to go. The two came into

RIGHT: *Waltrip's Daytona curse was in effect again in the 1982 season. The #11 team finished twentieth despite a sixth-place qualifying run. It didn't take him long to get back into the groove that year, though, as he won the Bristol and Atlanta races soon after.* BELOW: *The winning team in the 1981 pit crew competition poses with their hauler and car at Daytona in 1982.*

| 1982 Championship Standings				
Place	Car#	Driver	Car Type	Points
1	11	Darrell Waltrip	Buick	4,489
2	88	Bobby Allison	Buick	4,417
3	44	Terry Labonte	Buick	4,211
4	33	Harry Gant	Buick	3,877
5	43	Richard Petty	Pontiac	3,814
6	71	Dave Marcis	Buick	3,666
7	67	Buddy Arrington	Chrysler	3,642
8	47	Ron Bouchard	Buick	3,545
9	3	Ricky Rudd	Pontiac	3,537
10	98	Morgan Shepherd	Buick	3,451

Bobby Allison

Although nicknamed the "leader of the Alabama Gang," Bobby Allison was actually from Florida—he was born there, and that state was where he began his racing career. Allison's first appearance in a Grand National race came in 1961. By the mid-1960s, he was appearing regularly on the GN circuit and had landed a ride with Bud Moore for the 1967 season. Allison also raced for Cotton Owens and Mario Rossi before joining the famous Holman-Moody team in 1971. The #12 Coca-Cola team earned eleven wins that season.

At the start of the modern era, in 1972, the red-and-gold #12 moved over to Richard Howard, with Junior Johnson as crew chief. Their ten wins were good enough to earn them a second-place finish in the points standings. Setting the racing world on its ear, Allison piloted Roger Penske's AMC Matadors from 1974 through 1977. He liked the Matador so well that he used it to fill out the racing schedule with his own team during those years. The AMC wasn't taken very seriously by the racing community until Allison demonstrated its potential with five wins.

Allison rejoined owner Bud Moore for three seasons in the #15 Fords and Mercurys. He won his first Daytona 500 with the team, and garnered a total of fourteen victories.

Bobby spent the 1981 season with Harry Ranier in the #28. It was a successful partnership, but Allison finished second in the points once again. Allison spent the next four seasons with the DiGard team, finally hitting paydirt in 1983, when he took the #22 Miller team to the championship with six wins. The race was close yet again, but this time Allison beat rival Darrell Waltrip, edging him out by thirty-three points in the last race.

Allison and his sponsor moved to the Stavola Brothers team in 1986, running the #12 Buicks until midseason 1988. In a first-lap wreck at Pocono, Allison's crippled car was T-boned on the driver side by Jocko Maggiocomo. Allison was critically injured, and ended his racing career, but returned to NASCAR as a team owner, fielding the #12 for Hut Stricklin, Jimmy Spencer, Derrike Cope, and others.

Bobby Allison saw red figuratively as well as literally in 1983. Allison was a top-notch driver, third in all-time wins, but up to then had never found the chemistry to take him to a championship.

the final event only twenty-two points apart. Allison suffered blown tires and engine failure, finishing sixteenth to Waltrip's third. Waltrip had won his second championship.

Harry Gant had earned the nickname "Bridesmaid Harry" over the previous two seasons, capturing a pile of seconds but no wins. He finally made it to victory lane in 1982 in a battered Buick at Martinsville, and would earn his first superspeedway win later that year at Charlotte.

California driver Tim Richmond showed his talent in one of the (many) J.D. Stacy cars, putting together two wins. The #2 team's future was uncertain, though, and Richmond wisely moved on at the end of the year.

Bill Elliott had been running Winston Cup races since 1976, driving limited schedules with his family team. In 1982, Detroit industrialist Harry Melling, taking a chance on the talented young driver, backed the team. The #9 team logged eight top-fives, including several near-wins where they finished in second by car lengths.

Yarborough and Anderson found victory lane three times in their sixteen runs, but had different goals in 1983. Anderson wanted to run full-time for the championship, while Cale wanted to stick to part-time. When the team split up at the end of the season, and Anderson shut down his operation, Yarborough moved on to Harry Ranier's #28 car.

The Earnhardt-Childress team showed promise in 1981. At the end of the season, though, Childress did a noble thing: realizing that he didn't have the resources to match Earnhardt's talents, he turned Dale loose to find a better

ride. Earnhardt and Wrangler moved on to Bud Moore's #15 team, fielding Fords for the 1982 and 1983 seasons.

1983: Bobby Allison Wins the Title

Bobby Allison had been driving stock cars since 1961 and had been with some of the best teams around—Holman-Moody, Mario Rossi, Penske, Bud Moore, and Junior Johnson, among others. Although he had finished second in the points standings five times, he'd never won the title. In the two previous years he'd seen a midseason points lead gobbled up by "Jaws" Waltrip. This was even more frustrating for the DiGard team, who had parted unamicably with Waltrip in 1980. They were determined not to let Waltrip grab the title a third time.

Several important changes in 1983 gave DiGard what they felt was a good chance at the title. Replacing Gatorade, Miller Beer brought major sponsorship to the team. The car was changed from the green-and-white #88 to a red-and-white #22 (the Gatorade #88 moved to Cliff Stewart's team, with Geoffrey Bodine at the wheel). The team concentrated on improving its short-track package, the area where Waltrip had gained the most ground on them in 1981 and 1982. They also changed their late-season approach. The last two years they had gone into the stretch playing it conservatively, guarding a points lead. That hadn't worked, so they were determined to go for the win at every event, regardless of the points outlook.

From left: Team owner Harry Ranier, Cale Yarborough, and crew chief Waddell Wilson relax in victory lane at Daytona in 1983. Yarborough charged through the field for the win after starting at the back of the lineup. The team came back the next year with a repeat win.

The field was pretty even in 1983, with twelve different teams winning races and several competing closely for the title. Succesful drivers included Bill Elliott, who—with backing from Melling—was consistently competitive, leading the standings for part of the season and getting his first win in the season closer at Riverside. Richard Petty was back in form with three wins and a fourth-place finish in the points standings. Unfortunately, one of those wins came under suspicion when Petty was found to have a grossly oversized engine in the car. He was fined heavily but was allowed to keep the win.

Though Dale Earnhardt had three wins with Bud Moore in 1983, he was impatient over the team's progress with Ford's new T-Bird and engines. Rather than wait for the equipment to come up to speed, he returned to the Chevy camp, going back to Richard Childress' #3. Wrangler went with him, but also agreed to sponsor Ricky Rudd in Moore's car for 1984.

As the season moved into its second half, it again looked like a battle between Waltrip and Allison. Allison

led by 170 points, but Waltrip began whittling the lead down as they approached the short-track schedule. This was a familiar scenario, and most (including Waltrip himself) expected Waltrip to pull even and then take the lead. Allison, determined not to let another one slip by, pulled off a string of three wins in September. Bobby, leading by sixty-four points going into the closer, finished just a few spots behind Waltrip—close enough to retain a forty-seven-point lead. Allison and DiGard had finally achieved victory in NASCAR's premier series.

Neil Bonnett enjoys a quiet moment before a race in 1983. Bonnett provided Bob Rahilly and Butch Mock's Rahmoc team with their first Winston Cup win that year, but moved to a second Johnson-Hodgdon team in 1984.

1983 Championship Standings

Place	Car#	Driver	Car Type	Points
1	22	Bobby Allison	Buick	4,687
2	11	Darrell Waltrip	Chevy	4,620
3	9	Bill Elliott	Ford	4,279
4	43	Richard Petty	Pontiac	4,042
5	44	Terry Labonte	Chevy	4,004
6	75	Neil Bonnett	Chevy	3,842
7	33	Harry Gant	Buick	3,790
8	15	Dale Earnhardt	Ford	3,732
9	3	Ricky Rudd	Chevy	3,693
10	27	Tim Richmond	Pontiac	3,612

1984: The Iceman Winneth

There were lots of changes in the Winston Cup teams in the 1984 season. The biggest upheaval was when Richard Petty announced that he would leave RPE and drive for Mike Curb for the year. (Petty had not had much success the last couple of years running two cars from the shop.) In 1984, RPE would house only Kyle's #7 Ford, with 7-Eleven sponsorship. The Curb team never really crystallized, however, even though Petty posted two wins, the second of which came in spectacular fashion. Petty's two-hundredth came at Daytona in the July 4 race, with President Ronald Reagan watching as he and Yarborough crossed the line side by side. Though no one could have imagined it then, it was to be Petty's last win.

The points race was tight all year long, with no one sustaining more than a one-hundred-point lead at any time. Terry Labonte and Billy Hagan had picked up Dale Inman as crew chief for the #44. Though they would win only two races, Labonte's calm, consistent performance, which earned him the nickname "Iceman," put them in first place going into late summer.

Waltrip, chasing his third championship, was in the running for much of the year. Warren Hodgdon had come on as part owner of the Johnson team, bringing Neil Bonnet along in a second team car (#12), a situation Waltrip was never happy with. Budweiser—which had jumped over from the #44 team—sponsored both cars.

The "battle of the beers" heated up, with Coors putting its logo on Bill Elliott's #9. Elliott got his first superspeedway win and two others to again place third in points. Geoffrey Bodine was replaced in Cliff Stewart's #88 by rookie Rusty Wallace. Bodine went to the new #5 team of Rick Hendrick, a Charlotte-area car dealer, who saw his team pull off an upset win at Nashville in its first year on the scene.

As the season wound down, the points race narrowed to Labonte and Harry Gant. Gant had crept up in the points from eighth place, pulling into second after his win in the Southern 500. Going into the penultimate race, Labonte was only forty-nine points ahead. Fewer than 150 laps into the Atlanta race, Gant pulled into the pits with mechanical trouble and was behind the wall for eight laps. Gant came back out after repairs, and not long afterward Labonte was the one with trouble. The engine on the #44 car blew, relegating Labonte to a thirtieth-place finish.

Just when it looked as if Gant could pick up substantial points and perhaps take the lead, the pendulum swung again and his engine expired, setting him back to twenty-sixth. When the dust settled, Gant had picked up only a few points. Labonte, known as a top road racer, was able

to stay ahead of Gant in the season finale at Riverside, ultimately taking the championship by sixty-five points.

The season was marred by the death of rookie driver Terry Schoonover, who was killed in only his second Winston Cup race, when his #42 hit the retaining wall at Atlanta in October.

1984 Championship Standings

Place	Car#	Driver	Car Type	Points
1	44	Terry Labonte	Chevy	4,508
2	33	Harry Gant	Chevy	4,443
3	9	Bill Elliott	Ford	4,377
4	3	Dale Earnhardt	Chevy	4,265
5	11	Darrell Waltrip	Chevy	4,230
6	22	Bobby Allison	Buick	4,094
7	15	Ricky Rudd	Ford	3,918
8	12	Neil Bonnett	Chevy	3,802
9	5	Geoffrey Bodine	Chevy	3,734
10	43	Richard Petty	Pontiac	3,609

ABOVE: *Rick Hendrick (right) coaxed veteran crew chief Harry Hyde (left) into teaming with him and driver Geoff Bodine for Hendrick's Winston Cup debut in 1984. The #5 team scored three wins in their first year together.*

OPPOSITE TOP: *Terry Labonte shows the way in the 1984 Warren W. Hodgdon Carolina 500 at Rockingham. This would be one of the industrialist's last hurrahs in Winston Cup racing, as he hit serious financial troubles later that year.*

OPPOSITE BOTTOM: *As you might guess from the color scheme on the car, Marty Robbins took himself and his racing efforts with a touch of humor. The popular country and western singer was a Dodge man to the end (he died after the 1982 season), but changed his number to #36 in 1979 when Petty reclaimed the familial #42 for Kyle's debut.*

1 *While tires are being changed, the gas man loads two eleven-gallon cans of fuel into the car. A catch-can man keeps the overflow from spilling onto the track and discards the empty first can. Pit helpers also clean the car's grill and hand drinks to the driver.*

2 *For a four-tire stop the jackman first raises the side away from the pit wall (generally the right side, except on some road courses). A tire carrier delivers fresh rubber to the two tire-changers, who must be careful that the hose of their air wrench doesn't get caught under the car.*

Ballet in the Pits

One of the most exciting aspects of Winston Cup racing is the action in the pits. Teams can make pit stops "under green" or during a caution to fill up with gas, change tires, and make adjustments or minor repairs. Every second spent in the pits is precious, because it translates to time lost on the track or a loss of position in a restart after a yellow flag.

Early in the sport's history, few teams put much effort into honing pit-stop skills. It was the Wood Brothers who turned attention to pitting as a winning strategy, earning a reputation for bringing their drivers out ahead as a result of quick stops. Now, teams spend as much time practicing and preparing for pit stops as for any other aspect of their performance, and most pits now feature special cameras mounted on poles above the stall to tape stops for later review. Many teams have weight and exercise rooms at their shops to help crew members get in shape to handle the heavy gas cans, raise the car with one pump of the jack, or "triple lutz" around the front of a race car with tires and airwrench in hand.

A Winston Cup pit stop is a seven-member ballet, with each move precisely planned and choreographed for speed and efficiency. The actual size of the crew involved in a stop depends on the activity taking place. For a gas-only stop, three or four pit members go over the wall. For tire changes, the whole crew of seven participates. NASCAR generally limits the

LEFT: *Efficient pitting can frequently make the difference between winning and losing. Thanks to the heroic (and graceful!) efforts of his pit crew, Neil Bonnett won this race, the 1983 World 600, at Charlotte Motor Speedway. This is a photograph of his last pit stop before crossing the start/finish line ahead of the pack.*

3 *New tires go on and the old ones are set aside at the edge of the pit stall (the team is penalized if they roll out onto the pit road).*

4 *As soon as two lug nuts are on, the jackman drops that side and races around to repeat the process on the left. The tire changers follow after tightening all the nuts on the right.*

number of people involved to seven, but occasionally allows eight in special circumstances.

The time elapsed during the pit stop has steadily dropped over the years. In the 1960s, pit stop times of twenty seconds for two tires and thirty seconds for four tires were not unusual. By the mid-1990s, four-tire stops were down to sixteen seconds for the quickest teams. The speeds have jumped back up a bit over the last few years, since NASCAR limited the number of air wrenches that can be in use at any time to two. Twenty seconds for a four-tire stop has become the norm.

A big change in the conduct of pit stops came in 1991, when NASCAR imposed speed limits on pit row. Before then, cars raced full-speed down pit road, roaring into their stalls with crewmembers exposed just feet away. It was a dangerous situation that resulted in tragedy in 1990, when Ricky Rudd's #5 car went out of control entering the pits at Atlanta. He slammed into Bill Elliott's adjacent car, sending Elliott's jack-man flying. Mike Ritch, Elliott's tire changer, was caught between the two cars and crushed. His death led NASCAR to limit all cars entering or exiting pit lane to a prescribed speed, which varies from track to track. Based on the size and amount of space on pit road, the speed ranges from as low as 35 mph (56kph) on short tracks, to 65 mph (105kph) on some super-speedways. Any driver exceeding the speed limit is black-flagged and must return to the pits for a stop-and-go penalty. The limits have made pit lane much safer for the crews, but the slow speeds (relative to the cars on the track) put even more of a premium on fast-fast-fast stops.

Race crews have an opportunity each year to demonstrate just how fast they can be, in an annual pit crew competition held at Rockingham. Teams perform a timed four-tire stop, penalties are assessed (for example, for loose lug nuts), and the fastest team earns bragging rights for the year (and a little cash).

Pit Crew Competition Winners

(Note: competition switched from two- to four-tire changes in 1985)

Year	Team	Speed (seconds)
1967	The Wood Brothers #21	21.922
1968	The Wood Brothers #21	18.276
1969	Junior Johnson #98	21.947
1970	Mario Rossi #22	19.840
1971	cancelled due to weather	
1972	Howard-Johnson #12	22.600
1973	Nord Krauskopf #71	20.166
1974	Bobby Allison #12	19.828
1975	DiGard #88	18.021
1976	Richard Petty #43	19.689
1977	Richard Petty #43	17.390
1978	L.G. DeWitt #72	15.977
1979	Junior Johnson #11	16.261
1980	Richard Petty #43	17.089
1981	Wood Brothers #21	17.622
1982	M.C. Anderson #27	15.704
1983	Ron Benfield #98	14.689
1984	Junie Donlavey #90	15.456
1985	Richard Childress #3	28.898
1986	Richard Childress #3	27.601
1987	Richard Childress #3	23.831
1988	Richard Childress #3	23.808
1989	Rick Hendrick #17	24.681
1990	Harry Melling #9	24.002
1991	Bud Moore #15	22.565
1992	Rick Hendrick #25	23.142
1993	Roger Penske #2	22.454
1994	Rick Hendrick #24	19.363
1995	Junior Johnson #11	23.692
1996	Rick Hendrick #5	22.056
1997	Bill Elliott #94	20.870
1998	Richard Childress #31	20.460
1999	Joe Gibbs #18	19.166

LEFT: *The Kodiak team goes to work on Rusty Wallace's car in 1989. Good pit work helped the team to a championship that year. Here the crew performs repairs to the damaged sheet metal on the front right fender.* RIGHT: *How do the drivers ever find their pit stalls? Each crew waves a sign to guide its driver into the right slot. The superspeedways have spacious pit lanes and stalls, but at short tracks the pit boxes are tight. In the latter, cars must stop exactly —within the lines yet still leave enough angle so a driver can pull around the car pitting in front of him. Stalls are now determined by qualifying position, but before 1996 the defending champion always got first choice.*

Terry Labonte

Chapter Four

Pushing the Boundaries: 1985 to 1992

By the early 1980s, NASCAR's ledger book was solidly in the black. The organization had endured challenges to every facet of its operations and come out on top. It enjoyed financial backing from RJR and a plethora of new team sponsors, a tremendous pool of talent (young and old), and little direct competition in the marketplace. For all of that, however, NASCAR was still predominantly a regional sport in 1984.

Television coverage certainly brought many of the events into homes across the country, but viewers had to search long and hard to find race results, or any mention of stock car races, in newspapers outside of the Southeast. The sport still had a roughneck, grease-under-the-fingernails image and a limited fan base to match. Other than the periodic sensational Daytona 500 finish, NASCAR drivers and races were not making news nationwide. The 1985 season brought some surprises that began to change all that.

Winston Ups the Ante Between the expanding interest of corporate sponsors and R.J. Reynolds' escalating commitment to the points funds and Winners Circle programs, NASCAR and its teams were in pretty good

financial shape by the mid-1980s. Points money had quintupled since the Winston Cup's inception, with $500,000 paid out in 1984. At the 1984 awards banquet, RJR announced another hefty increase for the 1985 season, up to $750,000, with $250,000 for the series champion.

RJR felt, however, that the steady increase in funding, though substantial, wasn't garnering sufficient public attention. They remedied that at the end of the 1984 season with two breathtaking announcements.

The first was a Winston Cup all-star event. "The Winston" would be an annual, nonpoints race for all drivers who had won at least one race during the previous season. The field for the first running included twelve drivers, and the race was a seventy-five-lap event at the 1.5-mile (2.4km) Charlotte speedway. The purse was an astounding $500,000, with the winner taking home $200,000. This was a showcase event set for the same weekend as the Indy 500; needless to say, the Winston was heavily promoted.

And that was just the beginning. In today's world of $30 million-a-year basketball contracts, the concept of $1 million no longer has the impact it once had. But in

1985, a million bucks was a pretty impressive chunk of change. There were a number of drivers who'd earned that much in their careers: Petty had done so in the early 1970s, for instance, and Darrell Waltrip had come close to earning a million in each of the last few seasons. But what Reynolds proposed, in their second announcement, was a $1 million bonus purse. All a driver had to do was win three of four "prestige" races in a season. The designated races were the Daytona 500 (the most famous), the World 600 (the longest), the Winston 500 (the fastest), and the Southern 500 (the oldest). Any driver who won two out of the four would get a consolation prize of $100,000.

The prospect of earning a million bucks in one season was captivating all by itself—the idea of being handed that much all at once, at the end of one race, at a time when the richest purse was about $150,000, was simply incredible.

It didn't sound all that tough on the face of it—a driver just had to win three races. But Reynolds had done its homework, and knew that in the history of NASCAR only two drivers had ever won three of those four events in one

PAGE 102: *Terry Labonte, 1984's champion, replaced Darrell Waltrip in Junior Johnson's #11 in 1987. The team was solid but not spectacular and Labonte left to try his hand at ownership in 1990. The deal fell through, though, and he spent the year with Richard Jackson's Precision Racing #1 team.*
PAGE 103: *Winston Cup gas cans. Only one type of fuel is allowed in the series. Unocal 76 (not Gatorade as the nozzle caps might suggest) has been the only gasoline used by NASCAR through its entire modern era. The gasoline is rated at 104 octane, a special racing formula.*

season—LeeRoy Yarbrough in 1969 and David Pearson in 1976. And by 1985, there were many more competitive teams on the circuit, further decreasing the chance of anyone pulling off those wins. So RJR set the bar at just the right height, tantalizing fans and drivers with a goal that was attainable, but at odds that suggested that the tobacco giant needn't worry about paying up any time soon.

It turned out that RJR would have to pony up sooner than anyone expected. In one of those anomalies that give actuaries nightmares, the Winston Million was won in its very first year—not by one of the usual front-runners either, but by Bill Elliott, an up-and-comer who'd shown strength over the last few years in the #9 Ford.

Elliott had a storybook season, racing out of the backwoods of Georgia—"Awesome Bill from Dawsonville" was a song about him—to win eleven superspeedway events, despite missing two races due to a broken leg. He won the Daytona 500 and then the Winston 500 at Talladega, the first two of the four qualifying events for the award. Brake problems put him out of the World 600 at Charlotte, but he avoided technical problems and a few crashes that sidelined other front-runners and went on to win the Southern 500—and the largest purse ever awarded a racer up to then, $1,053,725.

As RJR had hoped, the event got massive publicity. The young redhead, in a snowstorm of dollar bills, made the front page of *Sports Illustrated* and his story was the highlight of every sporting news report. Elliott's total winnings for the year came to $2,383,000, a record that would last the rest of the decade.

RJR and NASCAR had sent their message loud and clear—the Winston Cup was no longer a poor cousin to other motorsports. It had the big purses and the big events to rival any auto racing series anywhere.

Rocket Science At the same time that RJR was pushing (and even shattering) the fiscal envelope with dramatically inflated purses, NASCAR was limiting track speeds and working to better ensure the drivers' safety.

Not surprisingly, race speeds had steadily increased over the years. Curtis Turner's pole qualifying speed for the 1950 Southern 500 was 82 mph (132kph). By 1971 the average qualifying speed was up to around 148 mph (238kph), and at Talladega, the circuit's fastest track, 187 mph (301kph). In 1982, Benny Parsons took the pole at the Winston 500 at an astounding 200 mph (322kph).

Ford released a new Thunderbird model and engine in 1983. By 1985, with help from a rule allowing Fords to sit an inch (2.5cm) lower than GM cars, the T-Bird had a decided speed advantage at the big tracks. At Daytona several Ford drivers posted qualifying speeds of more than 200 mph (322kph), with Bill Elliott at the top with an amazing 205 mph (330kph). The next closest competitor was Yarborough, at 204 mph (328kph). Elliott had his way with the field and easily won the race.

Bill's brother and crew chief Ernie Elliott had done extensive wind-tunnel testing with the T-Bird. They found that by making the car a few inches narrower (a measurement not covered by the NASCAR rulebook) it presented a smaller surface and decreased air resistance. At speeds in excess of 150 mph (241kph), air drag is as much of a factor in speed as engine horsepower, so reducing that drag gave Elliott an edge.

When they moved on to the Winston 500 at Talladega, Elliott's posted speed was truly awesome. He held his breath for a qualifying lap of just more than 209 mph (337kph). Holding his breath was probably a good idea, because the drawback of the body shaping that made the

OPPOSITE: *The 1986 Daytona 500: Bill Elliott had captured the pole at over 205 mph, but was taken out of the race in a crash. Geoffrey Bodine held on to beat Dale Earnhardt for his only Daytona win, after Earnhardt ran out of gas with only three laps to go.*
LEFT: *Drag racing ace Kenny Bernstein made a foray into Winston Cup racing in 1986, fielding Joe Ruttman behind the wheel of the colorful Quaker State Buick. Ruttman finished a solid second in this Richmond race. Kyle Petty won the race, his first Winston Cup victory.*

#9 so fast was that it also made it less stable. Poor handling is not the best quality in a car that is traveling at 209 mph. Only a pilot of Elliott's caliber could have kept that rocket under control.

Though the nearest competitor was going 4 mph (6.4kph) slower, Elliott did not pull away from the field at the beginning of the race. Then, on lap 48, an oil-fitting dislodged and the smoking car went nearly two laps down in the pits. Making up a lap in Winston Cup races is extremely difficult and almost always requires catching a

The field sorts itself out for a restart as it comes through the fourth turn at Rockingham in 1986. Morgan Shepherd, in the #75, led for several laps but finished twenty-fourth. Neil Bonnett (#12) took the win.

timely caution flag. On short tracks a dominant car might be able to make up a lap under green, but it's still tough. In the 1985 Winston 500, Elliott was nearly two laps down on a 2.66-mile (4.3km) track. Against all odds, though, he stormed back.

Consistently turning in laps of more than 204 mph (328kph), Elliott passed the front-runner twice to take the lead in the race in fewer than one hundred laps.

Elliott continued to turn out pole runs of more than 205 mph (330kph) at Daytona and Talladega that year, reaching the apex with a frightening speed of 212.8 mph (342.4kph) at the Winston 500 in 1987.

A Winston Cup car is aerodynamically designed to compensate for the effects of wind resistance and downforce. Basically, air flowing over the front keeps it glued to

the track, while the rear deck and spoiler do the same for the back end. That only works if the car is going forward, though. At the speeds teams were running in the mid-1980s, if a car presented any side other than its front to the wind—for example, if it spun out—air would catch under the surfaces that normally cause downforce and create lift instead. The car would literally become a flying wing, as air turbulence caused it to leap off the track.

When Bobby Allison's car took to the air in that same 1987 Talladega race and tore down the fence separating the fans from the track, NASCAR decided that the speeds had passed the limits of safety. Testing had shown that the cars, as designed, hit the edge of control at around 203 mph (327kph). NASCAR decided that the best way to reduce the chances of cars taking off was to reduce their

top speeds to below that mark. Beginning with the 1988 season, NASCAR mandated that a carburetor restrictor plate be used at Daytona and Talladega. The four events run at those tracks each year have since been known as the "restrictor plate races."

The effect was immediate. The 1988 Daytona pole speed dropped to 193 mph (311kph). As a result, Bill Elliott's lap speed of 212 mph (341kph) still stands as the stock car record.

The use of restrictor plates significantly changed the style of racing at those tracks. With horsepower restricted, individual cars could not pull away and run by themselves. Before the restrictor plates, if two cars were running together, the second car actually had the advantage: if it could pull up close to the leader, the air would pass over

both cars together. By running in the leader's "draft" the second car was towed in the slipstream and didn't have to run at full speed to stay with the car in front. At the chosen moment, the back car would pull out from behind, and the change in airflow would slow the lead car, allowing the follower to slingshot around to the lead.

With restrictor plates, the tactics changed. Long lines of cars drafting nose-to-tail can run faster than a single car or cars running side-by-side. As long as a car can stay in the draft, it can hitch a ride to the front, whether it is particularly strong or not. Thus, restrictor plate races are characterized by lines of cars running together in "freight trains" two, or sometimes three, vehicles wide. Drivers jockey for position, trying to get into the fastest line and avoid being "hung out" of the draft. Cars can go from first to twentieth place in one lap, then reverse positions in the next. Restrictor plate racing is as tight as you can get, and, because of the speed, drivers find it nerve-racking and draining.

Since most of the field is bunched together, accidents usually involve many cars. The 1996 Winston Select 500 at Talladega was an example. When the #6 and #24 cars touched on lap 129, it triggered a fourteen-car disaster that saw the #41 of Ricky Craven fly across the track. Masters of drafting, like Dale Earnhardt, play it like a chess game: they plan ahead, waiting for the perfect moment to make their move to the front.

Even with restrictor plates, the speeds at a number of tracks are fast enough to lift a car into the air if it is turned around. The sight of cars standing up on their noses then doing a dozen violent flips started to become far too common at tracks like Michigan and Pocono. To counter this tendency, a very effective safety device was instituted: a set of roof flaps on the cars. If a car turns around, the air catches under the flap and it springs straight up. The raised flaps act like ailerons on a plane—the air hitting them presses down on the car, keeping it on the ground.

Tire Wars

"Tires is what wins races" goes the saying. In the early years of NASCAR, racers used street tires or whatever they had lying around the shop. As races moved to paved tracks and become longer in duration, tire endurance began to play a factor in the outcome. Johnny Mantz clearly demonstrated this by bringing special tires to the first Southern 500. While everyone else spent precious time in the pits changing blown tires, Mantz went on to win by nine laps.

That performance attracted the attention of tire manufacturer Firestone, which had supplied tires for Indy cars. In 1955, they produced a special tire for stock car racing that was used almost exclusively for several years.

When Goodyear became involved in NASCAR in the 1960s, the two tire companies began to compete for the top drivers. By the end of the decade, Goodyear had captured the market and was the sole tire provider for NASCAR—other than a brief foray by McCreary Tires in 1979—through the late 1980s.

In 1988, a small Indiana company, Hoosier Tires, moved up from supplying the Sportsman Series to competing in the Winston Cup. Hoosier was able to pull off a number of successes, including winning nine races that

NASCAR conducts rigorous technical inspections to minimize the possibility of "creative rules interpretation." For each make of car NASCAR uses a body template to ensure that the shape of the car exactly fits the specifications. Small differences in slope or height can change the aerodynamics and confer an advantage on a superspeedway track.

A horrendous crash at Talladega in 1996 sidelined fourteen cars after Jeff Gordon and Mark Martin touched. Ricky Craven took the worst damage—flying across the track and over a pack of cars. Such pileups are a hazard in restrictor plate racing.

year. Since Goodyear had long been the sole source of rubber, it had been conservative in its formulas, focusing more on dependability than speed and performance. Hoosier caught them by surprise—though not for long.

The trouble with a "tire war" is that the emphasis shifts from having safe, solid tires to having the fastest product. The drivers, whose lives depended on reliable rubber, were openly fearful of the situation, and with good reason. A number of accidents caused by blown tires sent drivers to the hospital in 1988.

The battle continued in 1989, when Goodyear introduced a radial tire in April that was able to hold up longer at high speeds than the Hoosier bias-ply. The majority of teams moved back to Goodyear and Hoosier owner Bob Newton voluntarily withdrew from the sport. He had certainly put on a good show, as well as achieving far greater success than anyone had expected of the country's smallest tire company.

In the end, the drivers and teams, relieved to have the tire variable taken out of the racing equation, ended up with a better Goodyear product. It was back to the status quo—for a while.

At the beginning of the 1994 season, Hoosier announced that it was returning to Winston Cup racing. Through the previous year, the company had worked with an engineering and development firm and felt they had a product superior to any offering from Goodyear. In the words of Yogi Berra, it was déjà vu all over again. The Hoosiers proved to be fast in qualifying, and provided a definite advantage on some tracks, making them a godsend

Special Events: The Winston and the Busch Clash

In 1979, Busch Beer decided to expand its involvement in NASCAR by sponsoring a special race. The Busch Clash would be a non-points race held at Daytona, prior to the 500, for pole qualifiers from the previous season. In the spirit of qualifying, the race would be just a twenty-lap heat. Buddy Baker won the first Busch Clash, but Dale Earnhardt has been the master of the race, with six wins over the years. In 1997, the name of the race was changed to the Bud Shootout.

Another non-points race was inaugurated in 1985 as one of three headline-grabbing programs Winston announced for that year. The Winston (later known in turn as the Winston All-Star, Winston Select, and then again as the Winston) would be a short "run for the money" featuring drivers who had won at least one race in the previous season.

The format and location of the race changed a couple of times over the years. It was originally supposed to rotate among different tracks, but with Humpy Wheeler's expertise at racing promotion, the event soon settled in at Charlotte. After a couple of uncompetitive early races, the format was changed from a straight seventy-five-lap race to multiple segments, with the finishing order of the first races determining the starting lineup for the last part. In recent years, to add to the excitement, the finishing order of the first segment has been inverted for the start of the second. The winner of each segment received a purse, with the largest amount going to the victor of the last, ten-lap segment. The number of eligible drivers was expanded to twenty, including the nineteen most recent Winston Cup winners and a wild card. The wild card was determined by a heat race—the Winston Select Open—that was run for all drivers who didn't qualify for the Winston. The winner of the Open went on to race in the Winston.

Whether it's the prestige, the money, or just the chance to race fast and hard without worrying about points and the championship, teams and drivers have consistently gone all-out to score the Winston trophy, making this a race notable for many exciting finishes over the years.

The first running of The Winston was uneventful, however, until the very end. Harry Gant grabbed the lead at halfway and maintained a comfortable margin, though Darrell Waltrip started to close in near the end. With a few laps to go, Waltrip caught and passed Gant. As he took the checkered flag, the engine of the Bud #11 blew up dramatically. Rumor has it that ol' Junior Johnson ordered Waltrip to redline the engine as he passed the finish line, making sure to destroy it before the post-race inspection.

The 1987 Winston was a flashback to the fender-bending days of the 1950s. Earnhardt and Elliott engaged in several

scuffles during the race, punctuated by Earnhardt's famous "Pass in the Grass." Contact between the two near the end of the race sent Earnhardt's car into the infield, but he stood on the throttle and ended up in the lead and took the win.

Darrell Waltrip had been the resident bad guy with NASCAR fans for a few years, but he passed the baton to Rusty Wallace after the 1989 Winston. In the final ten-lap segment, Wallace tracked down the leader—Waltrip—and made contact as he started to move under him, sending Waltrip spinning. Waltrip was put at the back of the restart line (unfairly, he felt), and Wallace went on to win the race, though the fans roundly booed him as he received the trophy. The heat was finally off D.W.

The 1992 race was special for several reasons. First of all, it was the first Charlotte race to be run at night, under lights. Musco Lighting did an amazing job illuminating the 1.5-mile (2.4km) track to the satisfaction of fans and drivers alike. The race itself was slam-bang. Davey Allison won the first segment and was sent to the back to start the second, then worked his way up to sixth for the last ten-lap run. With seven laps left, Waltrip took a ride in the infield, bringing out a caution.

On the restart, Earnhardt jumped past Kyle Petty for the lead, while Allison moved up to third. Petty started back under Earnhardt, who rode him down to the inside of the track. Earnhardt didn't have the right angle going into the turn, though, and had to lift. Petty also lifted, to avoid contact, but Allison kept his foot in it and pulled up beside Petty going into the front-stretch dogleg. The two touched as they approached the checkered flag, and Allison's car spun around in front of the #42—taking the win as he hit the front straight wall in a blaze of sparks.

Earnhardt picked up the win in 1993, psyching out Mark Martin on a restart with two laps remaining. When Earnhardt grossly jumped the restart, NASCAR threw the yellow and lined them back up for another try. On the second shot, he was able to stay even with Martin into the turn and drove deep past him for the win.

Jeff Gordon inherited a win in the 1995 race when he backed out of a three-car sandwich, leaving Waltrip and Earnhardt to take each other up into the wall. Michael Waltrip did the same in 1996, earning his only Winston Cup win to date

by sliding under Terry Labonte and Earnhardt as they collided. Waltrip's win was also special in that he was in the Winston by virtue of winning the Winston Select Open heat race—the only time a wildcard entry has won the main event.

While the Winston started out as an adjunct to a Sunday Sportsmen's race in 1985, over the years the excitement and ferocity of the racing have made it a sellout event and a showcase for the best of NASCAR's talent.

OPPOSITE: *Dale Earnhardt poses with his first Winston trophy in 1987. His aggressive, full-throttle style of racing is well-suited to the short Winston's format.* BELOW: *In contrast, Jeff Burton and the #99 team acquired a reputation in 1999 for running well over long runs, climbing back from poor qualifying positions to challenge for the lead by the end of each race.*

Russ Wheeler's Chevy Lumina was the second entry in the two-car team depicted in the motion picture Days of Thunder. *Hardee's had been a longtime Winston Cup sponsor and although Wheeler was a "bad guy" in the movie, they took advantage of the opportunity to advertise on the big screen.*

for teams that needed a bit of an edge. Geoffrey Bodine's #7 team won five poles and three races using Hoosiers in its crucial first season.

Hoosier did not have a clear advantage overall, though, and by the end of the year most teams had again reverted to the tried-and-true strength of Goodyear Eagles. Bob Newton had mounted another strong challenge, but his small company couldn't outgun Goodyear.

Days of Thunder

Whether it was due to the publicity from "Million Dollar Bill" Elliott's incredible 1985 season or just coincidence, Hollywood decided it was time for another movie about stock car racing. *Days of Thunder*, released in 1990, was a big-budget film featuring top stars Tom Cruise, Robert Duvall, and Randy Quaid. The plot was loosely based on the story of multicar team owner Rick Hendrick. Cruise played a Tim Richmond-like character, Duvall a character based on veteran crew chief Harry Hyde. The movie included scenes based on real episodes from their relationship, such as a scene in which crew chief Harry Hogg has the driver run fifty laps hell-bent for leather, then fifty laps Hogg's way, and then compares tire wear. The film includes real racing footage. Several drivers (including Greg Sacks and Bobby Hamilton) were employed in making racing sequences for the film, and a number of racers had cameo appearances.

The public loved *Days of Thunder*, but racing insiders hated it. The movie depicted racers largely as egomaniacal Neanderthals, whose tactics for winning consist of intentionally wrecking the competition. In one famous scene, the bad boy on the circuit rear-ends the hero's car in his first race. When the hero complains to the crew chief, he's told, "No, he didn't slam into you, he didn't bump you, he didn't nudge you. He rubbed you. And rubbin', son, is racin'." This was the very image of stock car racers that NASCAR had been fighting for years. And while "rubbin'" was common in the early years of the sport, at the speeds achieved in the 1980s, intentionally hitting another car was more akin to attempted murder than smart racing. The NASCAR drivers had become professionals, and many were offended by their depiction in the movie.

Oddly, though, that presentation did nothing to hurt NASCAR's popularity. On the contrary, the movie gave racing a tremendous publicity boost. Millions of people who otherwise would never have heard of the sport were seduced by Cruise's charisma and by the movie's big-screen action and dramatic camera shots. *Days of Thunder* popularized stock car racing, and opened a new market to NASCAR: merchandising, the traditional offshoot of any major motion picture from *Star Wars* on. Today's massive NASCAR toy market sprouted from the products released for *Days of Thunder*.

1985: Awesome Bill Wins a Mill, but Jaws Takes the Title

It was a year of surprises. R.J. Reynolds started it out by announcing not only a significant increase in the points fund but also the Winston Race and the institution of the Winston Million award program.

The next surprise came at Daytona, and it was a harbinger of things to come over the course of the season, as Bill Elliott and the #9 team laid down blistering laps that left the competition shaking their heads. The Coors team had seemingly worked miracles on their Ford over the winter. Elliott, who had had four wins in all of his previous seasons, put together a dream year of eleven superspeedway poles and wins, breaking David Pearson's record. And Elliott became an overnight sensation when he won the Winston Million in its first year.

It started with a runaway win at Daytona, the first leg of the million-dollar award. A couple of wins later, Elliot pulled off the seemingly impossible feat of making up two laps at Talladega under the green flag to go on to victory. The win in the Winston 500 earned him $100,000 under the new award's guidelines. Elliott continued to pile up trophies but was unable to win the crucial World 600 at Charlotte, his first chance to nail the $1 million bonus. When Bill wasn't winning, he was often having trouble, so Elliott didn't move into the points lead until June, after his sixth victory. The next and last shot at the million came at Darlington, in the Southern 500. The race was by no means a runaway—Elliott beat Yarborough by only 0.6 seconds—but Awesome Bill was watched over by a guardian angel that day as he avoided crashes and mechanical problems that took out the toughest competition.

At that point, Elliott had a 206-point lead over Darrell Waltrip in the points standings. It looked like he'd have a perfect season, top dollars, and a title to boot. But something happened to the team after the Darlington win. It seemed as if they had been so focused on the Winston Million that once that was accomplished they considered their season over. Waltrip's season was not over, though, and once again he turned on the steam in the stretch. Elliott struggled just to place in the top-tens the rest of the year (except for his eleventh win, at Atlanta), while Waltrip picked up two wins and four more top-fives. Not only did Darrell catch the #9 team, but, as Elliott's crew watched dejectedly, he pulled ahead to a 101-point advantage. Elliott's amazing season ended on a sour note, as he relinquished the title to Waltrip.

Harry Gant came home third in points. Gant broke another string of frustrating second-places with wins at Dover and North Wilkesboro. While Elliott monopolized the superspeedway wins, Dale Earnhardt ruled the short tracks: the Wrangler #3 won both Bristol races and one each at Richmond and Martinsville. His success didn't come without controversy, though. Several drivers felt Earnhardt had driven to victory lane directly through their cars. Ricky Rudd laughingly commented on the situation at the awards banquet with a mock apology: "My shoes were shined when I got here but Dale Earnhardt ran all over them when he was coming up here to get his award." Neil Bonnett came home fourth with a pair of wins in the second Junior Johnson car.

Another surprise was an upset win in the Firecracker 400 by Greg Sacks, driving a DiGard research and development car. The win was tainted somewhat by allusions to an oversized engine that slipped by inspectors. Sacks' win also cast a shadow on Bobby Allison's relationship with DiGard, because Allison had struggled in 1985 and had

Legendary crew chief Harry Hyde calling the shots for the Miller team in 1989. Hyde worked with many top drivers, scored fifty-six wins in his career, and won a championship with Bobby Isaac in 1970. Hyde, who passed away in 1996, is perhaps best remembered as an innovator—always ready to apply new technology to race car setup.

achieved no wins that year. Allison took the contrasting performance of the R&D car as a slap in the face, and left for greener pastures.

Another veteran who had a less than stellar year was Richard Petty, in his second season with Mike Curb. The team was going nowhere fast: Petty was winless, had only one top-five, and finished fourteenth in the points. Kyle had moved from RPE to the Wood Brothers that year, so, for the first time in the history of NASCAR, Petty Enterprises was absent from most races.

1985 Championship Standings

Place	Car#	Driver	Car Type	Points
1	11	Darrell Waltrip	Chevy	4,292
2	9	Bill Elliott	Ford	4,191
3	33	Harry Gant	Chevy	4,033
4	12	Neil Bonnett	Chevy	3,902
5	5	Geoffrey Bodine	Chevy	3,862
6	15	Ricky Rudd	Ford	3,857
7	44	Terry Labonte	Chevy	3,683
8	3	Dale Earnhardt	Chevy	3,561
9	7	Kyle Petty	Ford	3,528
10	75	Lake Speed	Pontiac	3,507

Bobby Hillin Jr. pits the Stavola Brothers #8 Buick in 1985. The Stavola team added a second car in 1986, with Bobby Allison as the driver. Allison spent his last several years racing with the team, until he was sidelined by a crash in 1988.

1986: Winston Cup Says Good-Bye to Grand National

After 1985, the Winston Cup Grand National series would be no more. NASCAR announced that the series would be known simply as the Winston Cup beginning with the 1986 season. Although the media reps who routinely covered races talked about the "Winston Cup," television broadcasters and print journalists often dissented and used "Grand National" instead. Given their level of commitment to the series, RJR felt—and Bill France agreed—that Winston deserved explicit and sole recognition. With "Grand National" removed from the series name, the media would be forced to keep the "Winston" in Winston Cup reportage. The change caused quite a stir, raising allegations that NASCAR was more interested in selling cigarettes than in racing cars. Over the next few years, though, as it became evident that the change didn't signal a decline in the sport, the name "Winston Cup" came into common usage. At the same time, the name of the Sportsmen series (so called since its inception in 1950) was changed to the Busch Grand National series.

Another difference that was apparent from the start of the season was that Bill Elliott would not be repeating his phenomenal 1985 performance. Elliott was still running frighteningly fast qualifying laps (including the 212.8-mph [342.4kph] record he posted at Talladega), but the competition had caught up and he wasn't able to pull away from the field as he had the previous year.

The 1986 season featured thirteen winners—a new high in the modern era. Kyle Petty put the Wood Brothers back in victory lane with his first win, and Rusty Wallace got two wins with the Blue Max team. That ride opened up when Tim Richmond left to form a second team with Rick Hendrick. Geoffrey Bodine's Hendrick team was strong also, with a pair of wins and a top-ten points finish, but the combination of Richmond and mechanic Harry Hyde caught everyone's attention. The two had distinct approaches to racing and it took a while for them to work those differences out, but by the second half of the season it was clear that the team had superstar potential. Richmond was a tough, aggressive racer; with that energy channeled by Hyde, they were able to win seven races from June on. Richmond moved steadily up in the points, falling short of second place by only six points. The team was sure to be a player in 1987.

Bobby Allison moved to a second Stavola Brothers team for 1986, running alongside Bobby Hillin Jr.'s #8. Allison's #22 team won the Winston 500, setting a record of its own—not for speed but for age. At forty-eight, Allison was the oldest driver to win a Winston Cup race.

Greg Sacks gets set to go to work in the cockpit of the DiGard Miller American Buick in 1985. Sacks earned his sole win in 1985 in the July Daytona race.

The Stavolas won the other Talladega race as well, with Bobby Hillin. The win was Hillin's first victory, and it came in a race that saw twenty-seven leaders. Hillin's win came when he was just twenty-two, making him one of the youngest winners in Winston Cup history. Miller Brewery, which sponsored both Allison and Hillin, capitalized on the fact that they had both the oldest and (fudging the facts a bit) the youngest winning drivers on their team. The statisticians at Miller used the new math to celebrate another record as well: the brewery announced that the Miller American 400 race was Richard Petty's one-thousandth race (despite evidence that it was really number 999).

Dale Earnhardt and the Childress team took their victories beyond the short tracks and showed championship potential. Despite his five wins, Earnhardt unfortunately got more attention that year as "Ironhead" than as the champion. A hit on Darrell Waltrip at Richmond, combined with the previous season's complaints, forced NASCAR to censure Dale for reckless driving and levy a large fine. Earnhardt also started his tradition of just losing the Daytona 500 when he ran out of gas with only three laps to go. Regardless, the competent, focused efforts of the #3 team brought Earnhardt his second championship and Childress his first.

1986 Championship Standings

Place	Car#	Driver	Car Type	Points
1	3	Dale Earnhardt	Chevy	4,468
2	11	Darrell Waltrip	Chevy	4,180
3	25	Tim Richmond	Chevy	4,174
4	9	Bill Elliott	Ford	3.844
5	15	Ricky Rudd	Ford	3,823
6	27	Rusty Wallace	Pontiac	3,762
7	22	Bobby Allison	Buick	3,698
8	5	Geoffrey Bodine	Chevy	3,678
9	8	Bobby Hillin Jr.	Buick	3,546
10	7	Kyle Petty	Ford	3,537

Bill Elliott

In 1985, "Awesome" Bill Elliott burst into the limelight of Winston Cup racing and made headlines across the country. That was the year that Elliott won the Winston Million.

Elliott had been racing in the Winston Cup since 1976, when he started out with a family-run team. In 1982, he caught the attention of auto parts manufacturer Harry Melling, who assumed sponsorship for the #9. With Melling's backing, the team gradually gained momentum, winning its first race in 1983 and then setting racing on its ear in the amazing 1985 season. Elliott won eleven races and led the points race much of the year, before losing to Darrell Waltrip due to an end-of-season slump.

This was one of the fastest seasons in Winston Cup history. The Coors #9 Ford set records at many speedways, with four poles at speeds of more than 200 mph (322kph). In what is perhaps the most amazing show of strength in racing history, Elliott made up a two-lap deficit—without the help of a yellow flag—to win the spring race at Talladega.

And there was more to come. In 1987, Elliott became the fastest man in stock car racing, breaking his own record at Talladega with a pole lap at more than 212 mph (341kph). Since NASCAR mandated restrictor plates at the series' two fastest tracks starting in 1988, Elliott's qualifying lap of 212.8 mph (342.4kph) should stand as the fastest in Winston Cup racing for a long while. Elliott was also finally able to add consistency to speed in 1988, to win the Winston Cup championship.

After less successful seasons from 1989 to 1991, Elliott joined Junior Johnson's #11 team in 1992. The partnership started off with a bang, as Elliott won five races in 1992 and came in second in the championship, losing by only ten points to Alan Kulwicki in the last race of the season. After less impressive 1993 and 1994 seasons, Elliot once again decided to run his own team. His #94 team acquired top-notch sponsorship from McDonald's and finished eighth in the points in both 1995 and 1997 (a broken leg caused him to miss a number of races in 1996).

Bill Elliott has good reason to smile. His Coors Ford was the fastest thing on four wheels for several years in the mid-1980s. Here, Elliott gets the news that he won the pole for the 1985 Firecracker 400 at Daytona. His speed was 201.523 mph (324kph), quick enough to set a record for that race but nowhere near the 212-plus speeds he'd run later at Talladega.

OPPOSITE: *Darrell Waltrip pits the third Hendrick team car at Dover in 1987.*
LEFT: *Tim Richmond knew only one way to race—flat-out! Rick Hendrick paired him with veteran Harry Hyde in 1986 hoping the crew chief would temper Richmond's aggressiveness. Hyde later commented that owners always put him in role of mentor to young drivers when what he really wanted was a seasoned driver like Petty or Pearson to work with.*

The battle for Rookie of the Year was waged between two new teams. Alan Kulwicki, an ASA racer from Wisconsin, made the move to the Southeast and started his own #35 team with sponsorship from Quincy's Restaurants. Bahari Racing brought Michael Waltrip (Darrell's little brother) up from the Sportsmen series to race in the Winston Cup series in their #30. When the dust settled, Kulwicki won top honors as the newcomer in 1986.

1987: A New Allison Arrives While Tim Richmond Departs

Darrell Waltrip had won three championships with Junior Johnson, the most recent in 1985. About halfway through the 1986 season, Rick Hendrick approached Waltrip, making him a top-dollar offer to form a third team in his stable. Waltrip had been discussing salary with Johnson already, and when the driver took Hendrick's offer to Johnson, Junior made it clear that he wouldn't counter-offer. So, starting in 1987, D.W. was teamed with Waddell Wilson and Tide in the #17 Chevy. Despite Waddell's experience and credentials, the team was behind the curve on horsepower for much of the season, with only one win and a fourth-place finish in the points standings.

Terry Labonte moved to the #11 Budweiser ride, taking Waltrip's place. Billy Hagan's oil business had been on the ropes for a couple of years, and it was beginning to affect the race team. Johnson, reducing his efforts to one team (Bonnett moved on to the #75), felt Labonte had the right skills to earn them both another championship. The team was strong—one win, thirteen top-fives—but not

strong enough to chase down Earnhardt or Elliott. Johnson and Labonte finished third in points.

Cale Yarborough left Harry Ranier to form his own team. He bought Jack Beebe's operation, renumbered it #29, and put the Hardee's insignia on the car. This move left the #28 open, and Ranier turned to the youngest member of the Alabama Gang for a replacement: Bobby Allison's son Davey. The younger Allison had run a couple of races the previous season and was ready for a charge at Rookie of the Year. With considerable backing form Texaco, Allison had the most successful rookie season of any NASCAR driver. The team won two races, had nine top-fives, and finished twenty-first in the points, despite running only twenty-two races.

Davey's father's season in the #22 was notable as well, not so much for wins—he had one—but for a dramatic wreck that changed stock car racing forever. It occurred in the Winston 500 that featured Elliott's record-setting 212.8 mph (342.4kph) lap. Not long after the start of the race, Allison cut a tire, causing the car to spin around. The backward-pointing car had the aerodynamics of a kite, and consequently went flying up into the air. The car hit the fence above the front-stretch wall and pulled a section down as it tumbled along the straight. If momentum had carried the vehicle in another direction it could easily have landed in the crowded grandstands; as it was, the accident showered the crowd with debris, injuring several spectators. The fence was repaired, and the race finished (ironically, Davey won), but the incident made a deep impression on the NASCAR fraternity. The cars were clearly running beyond the boundaries of safety, for fans and drivers alike; starting in 1988, restrictor plates would be used at Daytona and Talladega to reduce the speeds.

Over the previous two years, Dale Earnhardt, crew chief Kirk Shelmerdine, and Richard Childress had strengthened their team piece by piece. Their improvement on superspeedways was enough to earn them the 1986 title. By 1987, the team was truly formidable: Dale scored eleven wins and was the points leader for almost the whole season. Elliott improved on his 1986 season, snagging six wins, but was unable to keep up with Earnhardt and finished a distant second, five hundred points behind.

Tim Richmond was the talk of NASCAR again in 1987—though not in the way he had hoped. In early December, Richmond came down with what appeared to be a severe flu, but the condition worsened and he ended up in the hospital with double pneumonia. Hendrick announced that Richmond would not start the season and appointed Benny Parsons as his replacement (in the #35, rather than #25, Folgers car). Richmond seemed to recover and returned to the circuit in June at Pocono. He showed that he hadn't lost his touch by qualifying third and pulling off an emotional win. It looked like he was back in top form when he won the next week at Riverside as well. By August, though, Tim's physical condition had deteriorated to the point that other drivers expressed concern about his ability to race safely. After the August Michigan race, Richmond retired from the ride, never to race again. Though he denied the rumors that he was infected with HIV, Richmond passed away of AIDS-related causes in August 1989.

Feelings toward Tim Richmond in the NASCAR community were complex. Many considered Tim to have somehow, through his flamboyant, public lifestyle and demise, betrayed the unwritten—and perhaps previously unexamined—mores of the sport. For others, though, Dale Earnhardt's simple summary had it right: "Tim Richmond was a helluva racer!"

1987 Championship Standings

Place	Car#	Driver	Car Type	Points
1	3	Dale Earnhardt	Chevy	4,696
2	9	Bill Elliott	Ford	4,207
3	11	Terry Labonte	Chevy	4,007
4	17	Darrell Waltrip	Chevy	3,911
5	27	Rusty Wallace	Pontiac	3,818
6	15	Ricky Rudd	Ford	3,742
7	21	Kyle Petty	Ford	3,737
8	43	Richard Petty	Pontiac	3,708
9	22	Bobby Allison	Buick	3,530
10	90	Ken Schrader	Ford	3,405

1988: Elliott Is Vindicated and Restrictor Plates Return

The year 1988 was a season of farewells for the NASCAR community. One of its longtime venues, the Riverside track, was slated to be torn up after the spring race. The old Richmond Fairgrounds track was on its way out as well, to be replaced by the three-quarter-mile (1.2km) Richmond International Raceway after the February race.

It would also be the last year for several familiar faces. Cale Yarborough hung up his helmet after 1988, ending a thirty-two-year career. It was Buddy Baker's last full season as well, after thirty years. Tragically, Bobby Allison's career ended when he sustained life-threatening injuries in an accident at Pocono. As Bobby's car spun across the track, he was hit by another car in the driver's door at full speed. Allison suffered long-term effects from the wreck, including the loss of the memory of a high point earlier in the year, when he and son Davey had finished first and second, respectively, in the Daytona 500.

That same Daytona saw Richard Petty involved in a horrific accident as well. Petty's car was lifted by contact with A.J. Foyt's and, catching the fence, the car disintegrated as it tumbled down the front stretch a dozen times. He was airlifted to a hospital, but his injuries proved to be minor.

Drivers also said good-bye to 210-mph (338kph) laps in 1988. With restrictor plates in force at Daytona and Talladega, the speeds dropped to well below 200 mph (322kph).

There were some pleasant surprises, too. Phil Parsons, Lake Speed, and Alan Kulwicki all won their first races—Kulwicki delighted the audience by reversing direction around the track for a "Polish victory lap" after his win. A race at the Phoenix International Speedway was added to the schedule, replacing the fall Riverside event and thereby maintaining a NASCAR presence west of the Mississippi. For the first time in many years, Goodyear faced competition in NASCAR when tiny Hoosier Tires convinced many teams to give its rubber a try. Hoosier doughnuts captured nine wins in the year but in the end the little company was unable to compete effectively against giant Goodyear. Hoosier dropped out at the beginning of 1989.

Ken Schrader and Benny Parsons swapped rides in 1988. Parsons had subbed for Tim Richmond, but Schrader was named driver of the #25 once it became clear that Richmond would not be returning. Parsons took over at Donlavey's #90 in his place.

A new team that attracted a lot of attention was Jack Rousch's #6. Rousch, who had been successful in IMSA and SCCA racing, received a number of top résumés when he let the word out that he'd field a Winston Cup team in 1988. His choice was Mark Martin, who had made a run at the Winston Cup in the early 1980s, but had fallen victim to Jim Stacy's stock car dabblings and returned to ASA racing. Observers who remembered Martin's focus and dedication expected him to make his mark (so to speak) with Rousch.

Several drivers made a serious stab at the 1988 title. Earnhardt, now "The Man in Black," with new sponsorship from GM Goodwrench, led the points standings from early in the season until June. Rusty Wallace had stayed within striking distance, however, and after a win at the last Riverside race ever, he took over the lead. Bill Elliott, a close second, was focused entirely on winning the championship. Wallace then stumbled in several races and, after a violent crash at Bristol, yielded the top spot to Elliott, who promptly scored five top-tens, including two wins, to build a buffer between himself and the second-place driver. Rusty wasn't about to give up, though: he won four of the last five races but couldn't catch the break he needed as Elliott finished close on his heels. Awesome Bill finally got his championship, by only twenty-four points over Wallace, and Earnhardt finished third.

1988 Championship Standings

Place	Car#	Driver	Car Type	Points
1	9	Bill Elliott	Ford	4,488
2	27	Rusty Wallace	Pontiac	4,464
3	3	Dale Earnhardt	Chevy	4,256
4	11	Terry Labonte	Chevy	4,007
5	25	Ken Schrader	Chevy	3,858
6	5	Geoffrey Bodine	Chevy	3,799
7	17	Darrell Waltrip	Chevy	3,764
8	28	Davey Allison	Ford	3,631
9	55	Phil Parsons	Olds	3,630
10	44	Sterling Marlin	Olds	3,621

Bobby Allison gets final words of encouragement from the crew before a race. 1988 was Allison's last year behind the wheel—he was critically injured at that year's Miller High Life 400 in Pocono, Pennsylvania, when a tire blowout sent him into the path of an oncoming car driven by Jocko Maggiocomo.

1989: Rusty Wallace Breaks Out

NASCAR's evolution continued in 1989. Benny Parsons moved from the cockpit to the broadcast booth, calling races for ESPN. Harry Ranier said good-bye to Winston Cup racing, selling his team to former engine builder Robert Yates. Hal Needham and Burt Reynolds sold their Mach 1 team as well. When Harry Gant took the #33 and Skoal sponsorship to Leo Jackson's new team, "Handsome Harry" quickly ended his long winless streak. Junior Johnson had been a Chevy "bowtie" man since he started his own team, but Ford wooed him away at the end of 1988, and Terry Labonte drove #11 Bud Fords in 1989. Early in the season, Chevy itself said good-bye—to the old workhorse Monte Carlo. Its replacement, the Lumina, was a strong contender right from the start; three of the top-five finishers in the points standings drove them.

Richard Petty was one of the few old-timers left on the circuit, but 1989 was not a good season for the King. His winless steak continued and he was unable to qualify for two races. Bill Elliott wasn't able to keep up his momentum from the previous year, and then he suffered a major setback: he broke his wrist in a practice accident, which handicapped him for the first part of the season. Earnhardt and Rusty Wallace both came out of the blocks fast and swapped the points lead between them for the first half of the year.

Overall, though, Darrell Waltrip was the attention-getter. His Hendrick #17 team showed its true potential when Waltrip won his first Daytona 500—in his seventeenth attempt. "This is the Daytona 500, isn't it? Please tell me it's the Daytona 500!" he clowned in victory lane.

The team put together a total of seven wins, good enough for fourth in the points and sufficient to put Darrell over the $10 million mark in career earnings—the first driver to hit that milestone. With a win in the Coca-Cola 600, he was eligible for the Winston Million but tangled with The Lady in Black (as Darlington Raceway is called) and came out the worse for it, unable to capitalize on the opportunity.

Earnhardt was at the top of the points column as the teams came to Charlotte, but a broken camshaft relegated him to the back of the field and Wallace took the lead. This despite internal dispute in the Blue Max team: Wallace was looking to get out of his contract and filed suit to do so. Owner Raymond Beadle didn't bite, though, and insisted on Wallace remaining. With Miller Beer signed on as a new sponsor for the next year, Wallace relented and the two renewed their association for another season. With that behind them, the team came on strong in the early autumn, while Dale ran into problems.

Mark Martin, a contender for much of the season, won his first race at Rockingham, moving him to second in points. The points race went down to Atlanta with Wallace leading Martin by seventy-eight points and Earnhardt by seventy-nine. The last race was a near disaster for Wallace, who at one point had to struggle back from thirty-third place. It wasn't pretty, but he managed fifteenth, enough for a twelve-point lead over Earnhardt, with Martin falling to third. Waltrip took fourth in the points, and Ken Schrader, who'd won his second race that year, placed fifth.

Amazingly, the Rookie of the Year was forty-seven-year-old Dick Trickle.

LEFT: *The drivers are not the only team members at risk on Sunday. Richard Petty's car backfired during a pit stop in the spring Atlanta race in 1989. The hot fumes ignited the gasoline being pumped into the car, setting gasman Robert Calicutt aflame. Calicutt suffered extensive burns from the horrible accident. As a result, today's gasmen wear flame-retardant uniforms and full-face helmets as protection.*
OPPOSITE: *Terry Labonte has a reputation as one of the better road racers in Winston Cup. Here he negotiates Junior Johnson's Ford through the esses at Watkin's Glen in 1989.*

1989 Championship Standings

Place	Car#	Driver	Car Type	Points
1	27	Rusty Wallace	Pontiac	4,176
2	3	Dale Earnhardt	Chevy	4,164
3	6	Mark Martin	Ford	4,053
4	17	Darrell Waltrip	Chevy	3,971
5	25	Ken Schrader	Chevy	3,876
6	9	Bill Elliott	Ford	3,774
7	33	Harry Gant	Olds	3,610
8	26	Ricky Rudd	Buick	3,608
9	5	Geoffrey Bodine	Chevy	3,600
10	11	Terry Labonte	Ford	3,589

1990: Martin Gives Earnhardt a Close Run for the Title

Dale Earnhardt had a very good 1989 season: he had focused on winning races and was successful five times. In pursuit of wins, though, he had put himself in a bind on more than one occasion and had lost the championship trophy as a result. The following year, 1990, saw a rededicated Earnhardt with an eye on the big, seasonlong championship picture. He started off the season with a roar, again coming close to a Daytona 500 victory—a victory snatched from him when he cut a tire while leading the last lap and Derrike Cope passed him by for his first Winston Cup win. The #3 team led in the points standings through the first part of the season but hit a slump in late spring, finishing outside the top-ten in four straight races.

Mark Martin demonstrated that his 1989 season had been no fluke, charging back from an initial deficit to take the points lead in the early summer. One reason he was down in the points early was a stiff penalty assessed against him after his Richmond win. Inspectors found illegal carb spacers and, while Martin was allowed to keep the win, it cost him forty-six points. Earnhardt wasn't far behind, though, and after a string of three wins in four

races (including a win in the July Daytona race, where he avoided a twenty-four-car wreck, the largest since 1960) the Man in Black moved ahead of Martin by one point. After a win at Phoenix, he was up by six points. Earnhardt had the clear advantage over Martin in the Atlanta finale, and the season ended with Dale up by twenty-six points, for his fourth Winston Cup championship. Martin gracefully did not comment on the forty-six-point penalty that had contributed to his loss.

Another record was set in 1990, when fourteen drivers won races, the most in the modern era. Derrike Cope backed up his Daytona win with a dominating performance at Dover. Brett Bodine, in drag racer Kenny Bernstein's #26 car, got his only career win, at North Wilkesboro. Rusty Wallace, with just two wins, was unable to repeat his success in the previous year, and split from the Blue Max team at the end of the season. Kyle Petty returned with Felix Sabates' #42 team and won the spring Rockingham race. (Owner Sabates rewarded him with a Rolls Royce.) Petty was on his way to sweeping that track with an autumn win as well, but succumbed to engine failure. The #42 seemed to have the bead on "The Rock," and would log several more wins at that track over the next few years. Harry Gant became the oldest

driver to win a Winston Cup race with his victory at Pocono. He topped Allison's record, winning at the age of fifty.

The 1990 season featured a game of musical chairs among the teams. It started when Terry Labonte left Junior Johnson to form his own team. Junior then tried to get Alan Kulwicki for the ride, but Kulwicki turned down a substantial offer to remain his own man. When Geoffrey Bodine got the seat instead, Ricky Rudd moved into the Hendrick #5. Brett Bodine took Rudd's #26 slot, and Morgan Shepherd moved into the #15. Another round saw Phil Parsons take Rick Wilson's seat in the Morgan-McClure #4 Kodak Chevy, only to be replaced himself by mid-March. Parsons was tough on the equipment, so the team hired Ernie Irvan. Irvan clearly had talent (he brought the team its first win at Bristol), but he could be overly aggressive, getting himself and others in hot water at times. After triggering wrecks that sidelined Neil Bonnett (and later Kyle Petty), NASCAR cautioned "Swervin' Irvan" to settle down. Dale Jarrett was replaced in the Yarborough car by Dick Trickle and moved on to substitute for the injured Bonnett in the #21 Wood Brothers Ford.

The Rookie of the Year award was given posthumously to Rob Moroso, who was killed in an accident on his way home after a race.

1990 Championship Standings

Place	Car#	Driver	Car Type	Points
1	3	Dale Earnhardt	Chevy	4,430
2	6	Mark Martin	Ford	4,404
3	11	Geoffrey Bodine	Ford	4,017
4	9	Bill Elliott	Ford	3,999
5	15	Morgan Shepherd	Ford	3,689
6	27	Rusty Wallace	Pontiac	3,676
7	5	Ricky Rudd	Chevy	3,601
8	7	Alan Kulwicki	Ford	3,599
9	4	Ernie Irvan	Chevy	3,593
10	25	Ken Schrader	Chevy	3,572

OPPOSITE: *"I don't think three races was a fair amount of time to judge" said Phil Parsons of his surprise release in 1990 from the Morgan-McClure team after only their third race together. Parsons had been involved in wrecks in all three of those races, but none was his fault.* BELOW: *Rudd, Bodine, and Elliott get turned the wrong way at North Wilkesboro in 1990. There was little damage, though, and all were able to continue the race. Kenny Wallace, seen slipping by the fracas in the #36 Pontiac, made his first Winston Cup start in this race.*

LEFT: *Derrike Cope follows up his Daytona 500 victory in 1990 with a commanding run at Dover in June. His Bob Whitcomb Chevy was at the front for ninety-three laps on the day.*
OPPOSITE TOP: *Longtime racer J.D. McDuffie lost his brakes going into the fifth turn at Watkin's Glen in 1991. The car picked up speed as it slid through the grass and flipped over upon contact with the tire barrier. McDuffie was killed in the crash.*
OPPOSITE BOTTOM: *Jimmy Means, whose car was also involved, frantically calls rescue workers to McDuffie's aid.*

1991: Earnhardt Makes It Five as the Skoal Bandit Becomes "Mr. September"

If the competition thought Dale Earnhardt was tough in 1990, they were in for more of the same in 1991. The RCR team added consistency to its repertoire, and, even with only four wins, they weren't seriously challenged for the lead all year. Ricky Rudd was the closest competition, finishing second with one or two wins—depending on whom you ask. Rudd won the race at Sears Point, but was later stripped of the win by NASCAR because he got into Davey Allison on the last lap, sending Allison spinning. Rudd finished first and Allison second, but NASCAR switched the order for the records. Allison had a great season, with five wins and a third-place finish in points.

The sensation of the year, however, was "old man" Harry Gant. Gant got a win on the strength of fuel efficiency in the Winston 500 (some say aided by an illegal last-lap push from Skoal teammate Rick Mast), but was in twelfth place in the points in late summer. Crew chief Andy Petree, who had been doing some experimenting with the camber on the car, hit on a winning formula. Gant went on to beat Davey Allison in the Southern 500, winning the $100,000 Winston Million two-out-of-four prize. Gant then took the lead from Allison at the end of the next race, at Richmond, eventually winning that as well.

There was no late-race pass at the next race, in Dover. Gant dominated, ending up lapping the field on his way to three victories in a row. By the time the circuit rolled around to Martinsville, everyone was rooting for the popular driver. Gant looked like he might make it four in a row at Martinsville—until Rusty Wallace sent him spinning about two-thirds of the way through the race. Gant was able to stay on the tail end of the lead lap, though, and engineered an amazing comeback that had him passing everyone to retake the lead in his damaged Olds on lap 454. At North Wilkesboro, Gant looked like he'd break the modern-era record and score his fifth straight win; he led the whole race until a ten-cent part broke, leaving him with no brakes. Earnhardt was able to slip past him with just nine laps left, and broke the streak. By virtue of his four in a row, Gant moved up to fourth in the points chase.

Dale Jarrett earned his first win at Michigan in a squeaker that had Jarrett and Davey Allison running the last two laps side by side, with Jarrett winning by a nose. Ernie Irvan's team was strong as well, taking the season opener at Daytona 500 and also winning at Watkins Glen. The Watkins Glen race was marred by the death of longtime independent J.D. McDuffie. McDuffie's #70 lost control going into the sharp number five turn and hit the tire barrier at full speed. The fifty-three-year-old racer had been a Winston Cup regular since 1963 and had run 653 races.

Another death, at the final Atlanta race the previous year, triggered major overhauls in pit-stop procedures.

1991 Championship Standings

Place	Car#	Driver	Car Type	Points
1	3	Dale Earnhardt	Chevy	4,287
2	5	Ricky Rudd	Chevy	4,092
3	28	Davey Allison	Ford	4,088
4	33	Harry Gant	Olds	3,985
5	4	Ernie Irvan	Chevy	3,925
6	6	Mark Martin	Ford	3,914
7	22	Sterling Marlin	Ford	3,839
8	17	Darrell Waltrip	Chevy	3,711
9	25	Ken Schrader	Chevy	3,690
10	2	Rusty Wallace	Pontiac	3,582

LEFT: *Darrell Waltrip thought that the end of the 1990 season might be a good time to try fielding his own team. The #17 team's sponsor, Tide, agreed, so Ricky Rudd replaced Waltrip. D.W.'s new team won five races in the first two years but struggled thereafter.* BELOW: *Jeff Gordon was still an unknown to the Winston Cup world in 1991. He had moved from sprint cars to the Busch Grand National series and was running with Bill Davis' Ford team. His performance had started to raise eyebrows, and Davis was planning to move the team to Winston Cup. To everyone's surprise, Gordon signed instead with a third Hendrick Chevy team for 1993. Gordon did run in the last race in 1992, which also was Richard Petty's final Winston Cup appearance.*

Ricky Rudd lost control coming into the pits at full speed and slammed into Bill Elliott's car. Elliott's tire changer was caught between the cars and killed. NASCAR tried several approaches to improve pit road safety, finally settling on speed limits.

There were some interesting team changes in 1991. Junior Johnson again expanded his operation to two cars, and tried once more to get Alan Kulwicki for his team. Kulwicki, however, had what he thought was a deal with Maxwell House for sponsorship, and again declined. Some weeks later, Johnson announced Sterling Marlin as his second driver—and Maxwell House as the sponsor. Kulwicki was stuck with a blank car.

This was the year of Desert Storm, the war against Iraq, and RJR wanted to honor the U.S. armed forces by backing five cars in the Daytona 500 with Army, Navy, Marines, Air Force, and Coast Guard paint schemes. Kulwicki was asked to paint his car with a camo-colored U.S. Army scheme. The car was a dog-ugly tan and olive, but so unusual that it attracted a lot of attention. Those taking a close look included the executives of Hooters restaurants, who signed on as Kulwicki's sponsor later that year.

In a sense, Johnson actually ran a third car in 1991. After the Winston, Johnson's #11 was found to have an oversized engine; Johnson was fined and suspended from four races. To keep sponsor Budweiser on the track, Johnson's wife Flossie was listed as the car owner, and the number was changed to #97 for the proscribed events.

Darrell Waltrip made another career move, leaving the Tide ride to start his own #17 team with Western Auto as sponsor. He won two races in his first year as owner and driver and perfected a Jekyll-and-Hyde routine for the television cameras, in which the "owner" would comment on the performance of his "driver" and vice versa.

1992: The King Says Good-Bye as the Underdog Proves a Point

Richard Petty's career in NASCAR spanned five decades. For most of that time he had been extraordinarily successful, amassing records for wins and championships that might never be equaled. Since the mid-1980s, though, the King's fortunes had waned. Winless since 1984 and with standings consistently outside the top-twenty, Petty, deciding it was time for a change, announced that 1992 would be his last season as a driver. To honor his legions of loyal fans, he would designate the season a "Fan Appreciation Tour," which would feature numerous public appearances and special merchandise and events. Fans were treated to a taste of the old Petty at the July Daytona race, roaring their approval as he led the beginning of the race.

A final farewell took place with the passing of NASCAR's founder, "Big Bill" France. Bill Sr. had been seriously ill for several years, and on June 7 he died, at the age of eighty-two. Another old friend who left the scene in 1992 was Dick Beatty, NASCAR's chief inspector, who retired at the end of 1991. In choosing Beatty's replacement, NASCAR adopted a "takes a thief to catch a thief" approach, appointing Gary Nelson, one of the more "creative" crew chiefs, to the position. Nelson's unbending but impartial attitude was widely lauded in the garages.

The 1992 championship played out among three teams. Davey Allison and the Yates #28 were at the top of their

---

R.J. Reynolds backed five unsponsored drivers in the 1991 Daytona 500, painting their cars with the colors of the branches of the U.S. military. Here, Micky Gibbs' #24, Greg Sacks' #18, Alan Kulwicki's #7, Buddy Baker's #88 and Dave Marcis' #71 pose in formation on pit road prior to the race.

1992 Championship Standings

Place	Car#	Driver	Car Type	Points
1	7	Alan Kulwicki	Ford	4,078
2	11	Bill Elliott	Ford	4,068
3	28	Davey Allison	Ford	4,015
4	33	Harry Gant	Chevy	3,955
5	42	Kyle Petty	Pontiac	3,945
6	6	Mark Martin	Ford	3,887
7	5	Ricky Rudd	Chevy	3,735
8	94	Terry Labonte	Chevy	3,674
9	17	Darrell Waltrip	Chevy	3,659
10	22	Sterling Marlin	Ford	3,603

game: Allison won a popular Daytona 500 victory and had the early points lead. The last two years had not been stellar for Bill Elliott, who not only drove but was beset with the pressure of helping to run the #9 team. In 1992, Elliott left for Junior Johnson's fabled #11 to be "just the driver." They immediately produced results, winning four races in a row following Daytona. Even so, Elliott was unable to wrest the points lead from Allison.

Allison held onto the lead until the summer, with Gant, Elliott, and Kulwicki vying for the spots immediately behind him. When Davey was injured in an end-over-end accident at Pocono, Elliott moved into the lead. He remained at the top for most of the rest of the season, expanding his lead to 154 points after Darlington in September. That gap dwindled over the next five races, however, as Elliott suffered problems. Going into the final race, Allison had the lead by thirty points over Kulwicki and forty points over Elliott.

Actually, there were six drivers who had a mathematical chance at the title by the time of the Atlanta race. Gant was in fourth place with two wins (extending his record of oldest winner to the current mark of fifty-two), and Mark Martin and Kyle Petty were not far behind. Those three all struggled in Atlanta, leaving the #28, #7, and #11 to duke it out for the title. Allison was running in fifth, safely in the points lead, when he was caught up in an accident and taken out of the race. It was down to Kulwicki and Elliott.

The adage "won the battle but lost the war" applied in spades at Atlanta. Elliott won the race, but lost the championship by ten points. Smart pit strategy by the #7's Paul Andrews kept Kulwicki on the track, to lead the most laps in the race. That bonus, combined with Kulwicki's second-place finish, was enough to keep him ten points up for the title. If Elliott had led by one more lap, he would have had the most-laps-led bonus, and the two would have been tied in the points. Elliott would then have won the tie by virtue of having won more races.

Kulwicki had altered the nameplate on the front of his Thunderbird to read "Underbird." The independent underdog was vindicated in his decision to stay with his own team, and once again delighted the fans by celebrating the accomplishment with his patented "Polish victory lap."

The King's last hurrah. The crowd at the 1992 Firecracker 400 was delighted to see Richard Petty qualify on the front row. Sterling Marlin was roundly booed when he knocked Petty off of the pole, and asked reporters if they thought he'd need security guards at a publicity session he was about to attend. Petty gave the crowd a reason to cheer at the start of the race, though, taking the point from Marlin and leading the first five laps.

Big-Time Sponsors

Somewhat to its detriment in terms of public perception, NASCAR's biggest sponsor tie-ins have been with tobacco and beer companies. Up until the 1980s, however, sponsorship tended to come from companies selling automotive products (oil, parts, services), soft drinks, or fast food. Sponsors pegged the NASCAR audience as southern white males and invested according to the interests of that demographic group.

In the late 1980s, the market began to broaden. Companies like Tide and Kodak took a chance on the market research, promoting general consumer products through NASCAR. Their success and long-lasting commitment helped entice an even greater variety of corporations into promoting through Winston Cup. By the mid-1990s toy companies (Hot Wheels), cereal companies (Kellogg's), cable television networks (the Family Channel and Cartoon Network), and telephone services (Bell South and Close Call) were sponsoring cars. Showing just how eclectic NASCAR has become, Patty Moise's Busch Grand National car has been sponsored by Rhodes condoms the past few seasons.

Following is a list of some of the big-name sponsors in Winston Cup racing.

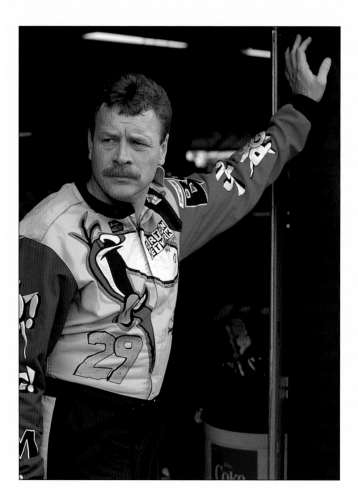

Folger's
Coffee is a general consumer product that has become an object of on-track competition. In its battle for market share, Folger has gone up against Maxwell House on the racetracks of the Winston Cup circuit, sponsoring top cars for Rick Hendrick and Jack Rousch.

Ford
In order to promote its Motorcraft line of parts and credit service, Ford sponsored Bud Moore's #15 Ford from 1985 to 1995, then Robert Yates' #88.

Hardee's
Southern fried chicken was a natural tie-in with stock car racing, and Hardee's has been part of the scene for many years.

Kodak
Kodak films are another broad-target consumer product that has successfully promoted through NASCAR. Kodak has worked with the Morgan-McClure team through most of the latter's tenure in Winston Cup racing and has had front-running teams with Ernie Irvan, Sterling Marlin, and Bobby Hamilton at the wheel.

Tide
Tide's sponsorship was a significant step for NASCAR: they were the first company to put big money into NASCAR that was associated neither with automobiles nor with selling products oriented to southern men. Tide's Day-Glo colors are among the most recognizable and familiar to NASCAR fans, and the Tide teams have enjoyed considerable success.

Valvoline
Valvoline, which has sponsored Winston Cup teams since the early 1980s, was one of the first of many oil companies to enter the market. Many top drivers have enjoyed Valvoline backing.

LEFT: *Taking advantage of an increasing family orientation in NASCAR, the Cartoon Network began sponsoring Winston Cup cars in 1996. Robert Pressley, seen here in the colorful uniform, replaced Steve Grissom in the #29 ride later that year.* OPPOSITE: *Texaco has had a successful relationship with Robert Yates (and Harry Ranier before him) since 1987. In 1994 Dale Jarrett replaced the injured Ernie Irvan in the Texaco #28 car. When Ernie returned to the circuit for several races at the end of that year, Texaco put their star on a second Yates car for him.*

Chapter Five

In the Limelight: 1993 to Today

History seems to divide itself naturally into eras. Great events or great leaders characterize a period of time, forming its unique place in the whole. NASCAR's history is no exception. Early on, stock car racing was about fast cars, and which model could be pushed the hardest and last the longest: Lincoln versus Buick versus Hudson and so on. Men like Edward Glenn "Fireball" Roberts and Richard Petty changed that focus. The men and women behind the wheel—the racers—became the heroes. Their grit and determination and their skill at wrestling their metal behemoths around a turn at the edge of control were what fans came to see. Since then, the history of NASCAR has been the history of its heroes and champions—of Petty, Pearson, Yarborough, Waltrip, Earnhardt, and Elliott, to name a few. Each had his era, a time when his style and personality defined what NASCAR was all about. In 1993 NASCAR and the Winston Cup entered a new era. Its new heroes—Jeff Gordon, Bobby Labonte, Dale Jarrett, and many others—brought a new look and an unprecedented level of popularity to the series.

Over the second half of the 1990s, NASCAR reached a pinnacle of success. It has become the fastest-growing and

most popular sport (in terms of attendance and television viewership) in the United States. The series has added new venues—Texas, Las Vegas, California—and the old familiar tracks have continuously expanded to accommodate the swell of fans. Many Winston Cup tracks seat well over 100,000 people, and events are routinely sold out. When the circuit rolls around to the Richmond International Speedway twice a year, the crowds gathered there make it the third largest city in Virginia.

One way to gauge the popularity of a sport is to look at the health of its merchandise market. NASCAR merchandising is in full bloom. Fans can get anything they want featuring their favorite driver, from the traditional T-shirts and baseball caps to toy cars, action figures, collectible cards, even knives and plates.

Why is Winston Cup racing so popular now? The same things that made it work in 1950—so wisely recognized by Big Bill France—have taken it to the top today. Namely, fans identify with the drivers and the cars. Despite obvious alterations, Jeremy Mayfield's #12 Ford is still recognizable as a Taurus, a car that millions of Americans own and drive. More important, NASCAR drivers have

made it their priority to remain in touch with the fans. Although they are an elite class of athletes, they don't act that way. Many people would feel a bit awkward sitting down to chat with a Nigel Mansel or Alex Zanardi, but Mark Martin and Ken Schrader practically feel like members of the family. More so than in any other sport, NASCAR drivers are accessible to the fans and let the fans know they are appreciated. The first rule an aspiring Winston Cup driver learns from his peers is that the fans are the reason the drivers are there, not the other way around. You never charge for an autograph, and you give back to the community. NASCAR stars like Kyle Petty, Morgan Shepherd, and Ray Evernham put their hearts as much into the charity events they organize and sponsor as they do into their yearly quests for the championship.

Today's NASCAR drivers and crew chiefs are the heroes of millions of fans in every demographic category. When all the members of a family—from grandpap to mom and dad and baby sister—can enjoy the same sporting event, you have a winner. One reason for the Winston Cup growth spurt of the mid-1990s, was the emergence of young, clean-cut drivers—downright heartthrobs like Jeff Gordon and Bobby Labonte, for instance—who made stock car racing appealing to a previously underdeveloped market segment: young girls.

The Winston Cup's success certainly goes beyond good looks and charisma, though. Without exception, the folks in NASCAR demonstrate an amazing work ethic and sense of responsibility. Drivers racing at 190 mph (304.7kph) need to take responsibility for their actions. Not that there isn't some finger-pointing (these are human beings after all), but the NASCAR team members clearly adhere to the maxim that you make your own luck, good or bad. No one in the Winston Cup garage expects a free lunch. In a world where sports figures are seen on the news as often for their extra-legal highjinks as they are for highlight-reel performances, you can depend on NASCAR's drivers to be upstanding.

While the money in Winston Cup is now on a par with that of any top professional sport—multimillion-

PAGE 134: *Terry Labonte leads teammate Jeff Gordon at the start of the Goodwrench 400 at Rockingham in 1996. Both drivers suffered engine problems that day and finished at the back of the pack.* PAGE 135: *Beyond a team's main sponsor and one or two associate sponsors, each team carries dozens of smaller sponsor decals on their car. Many of these companies back special awards or benefits programs.* LEFT: *The Joe Gibbs teams frequently ran together at the front of the field in the 1999 season. Rookie sensation Tony Stewart, in the orange #20 car, won Rookie of the Year honors and three races, and had the highest finishing position in the points standings of any Winston Cup rookie ever.*

Dale Earnhardt's 1998 Daytona 500 win was so long in coming that even the "anybody but Earnhardt" contingent couldn't begrudge him the victory. Earnhardt was honored with an unprecedented gesture by the Winston Cup community as all of the teams lined up along pit road to congratulate him as he drove to the winner's circle.

An International Event In the 1950s, as NASCAR was branching out of the nebula of rural short tracks all over the eastern half of the United States, the Grand National schedule regularly encompassed forty to fifty events at nearly as many different locations. With the inception of the Winston Cup, the series was trimmed down to thirty or fewer races, almost all in the Southeast. In the 1990s, as interest in NASCAR has expanded, the schedule has again grown, and now includes venues in many major markets across the nation. When the Ontario, California, track closed, NASCAR added Phoenix to retain a presence in the Southwest. New Hampshire Speedway took the series into the heart of a thriving Busch North Division racing community. The Las Vegas, Texas, and California speedways are all part of this strategy of filling the gaps in NASCAR coverage across the country.

Not only are the locales of the races changing, but the character of the races and tracks are different as well. NASCAR grew up on the short tracks, but today the speed, excitement, and seating capacity of speedways 1.5 miles (2.4km) or longer have shifted attention away from the bullrings. With the closing of North Wilkesboro in 1996, only six short-track events remain on the schedule, including the races at Richmond, which, technically, is a superspeedway. NASCAR recognizes that fans still love short-track races, but with the economic realities faced by track owners, the vivid image of brake rotors glowing cherry-red as drivers repeatedly slam on the binders in the turns may go the way of rooster-tails of dust kicked up behind the dirt-trackers.

In 1996, NASCAR began an experiment with international racing, although this wasn't the first time that Winston Cup drivers had gone overseas to run stock cars. When the ThunderDome race track opened near Melbourne, Australia, in 1988, a handful of Winston Cup drivers—including Bobby Allison, Kyle Petty, Neil Bonnett, and Dave Marcis—flew over for the inaugural race. Over the past three years, many of the luminaries from the Winston Cup, Busch Grand National, and Craftsman Truck series have flown to Japan for a postseason exhibition race. The non-points event was held at the Suzuka Circuitland road course the first two years, then at an oval track, the Motegi Thunder Special, in 1998. Japanese race fans offered a warm welcome to the NASCAR drivers and crews, leading to speculation about expansion of international efforts. Back home, however, the reception wasn't quite as warm; many teams and fans felt that with the number of tracks and areas of the United States still looking for Winston Cup race dates, the schedule shouldn't be diluted with efforts outside the country.

dollar seasons are not uncommon—there's a difference in the way that money is earned. In many sports the players get their multimillion-dollar, multiyear contract before they perform, and retain those contracts regardless of their performance. NASCAR drivers in large part earn their pay week to week. As in the real world, if they don't do the job they were hired for, they don't get the money.

These factors have all helped to make Winston Cup the United States' premier sporting series and a household name. Five years ago, being a NASCAR fan in Pittsburgh was something like belonging to a secret society. Today, fans can get Sunday's race results from the minimart clerk down the street or compare favorite drivers—identified by a flag hanging in the yard or a poster on the office wall—with neighbors and coworkers.

Where Do We Go from Here? Having
reached the level of success the sport now enjoys, where
will it go over the next decade or two—or five? Fans can
definitely expect continued expansion, both within the
Winston Cup and in the other series that run at the top
levels. After many years with two top divisions, the
Winston Cup and the Busch Grand National division,
in 1993 NASCAR added the Craftsman Truck series.
Launched in response to the phenomenal sales of pickups
in the early 1990s, the series was initially well received.
Whether because the market is saturated or—as occurred
with the convertible division in the 1950s, the trucks don't
differentiate themselves sufficiently—the series' popularity
hasn't grown as expected. Nevertheless, it provides additional opportunities and a solid proving ground for drivers
working toward the Busch and Winston Cup.

One thing stock car fans can always count on is that
the pendulum of change will swing. In the early days of the
sport there were a few perennial contenders with factory
backing, while the remainder of the field were also-rans.
The number of competitive teams expanded dramatically
through the 1970s and into the 1990s. With the predomi-
nance of large, multicar teams in the late 1990s, though,
is NASCAR returning to a bipolar state after its fiftieth
anniversary? The next few years will be telling for teams
on both ends of the spectrum—the five-car Rousch Racing
stable as well as such single-car operations as Dave Marcis'
and Butch Mock's.

The face of NASCAR has changed as well. Gone is
the scruffy, grease-monkey-cum-driver in victory lane and
the hard-fighting, hard-charging southern rascal. While
the advent of the clean-cut, courteous driver-as-sponsor's-
representative has its upside for the sport, it would be a
shame if NASCAR completely lost the grit and down-home
character that made it what it is—and differentiated it for
so many years from other motorsports.

NASCAR will soon face another succession as well,
once the firm guidance of two generations of Bill Frances
comes to an end. Will the next leader be able to live up to
the task? Jim France, Bill's younger brother, is the president
of International Speedway Corporation and executive vice-
president of NASCAR. Bill's son, Brian, is NASCAR vice-
president of marketing and communication. The two have
been integral to NASCAR's growth and development for
years and represent another generation of leadership and
stability for the organization. But the France family is not
the only source of leadership. Track and team owners
Roger Penske and O. Bruton Smith, major forces in
NASCAR over the years, have the vision and presence
to help direct the sanctioning body, if called upon.

Although crystal-ball gazing has always been a popular
pastime among NASCAR aficionados, with the unexpected
twists and turns we've seen over the course of the sport's
history, the only prediction that all of the pundits would
probably agree on is that NASCAR and Winston Cup
racing will continue to excite and surprise observers for
many years to come. Hopefully, we—and our children
and grandchildren—will have the opportunity to someday
call these "the old days" and reflect on the achievements
of the second half-century of NASCAR stock car racing.

*Richard Petty watches his car from the pits in 1997. Petty
Enterprises is the oldest team on the NASCAR circuit. In fact,
there's been a Petty-owned car run every season (though not
always a car driven by a Petty) of NASCAR's history.*

1993: A Year of Loss

The accomplishments of the 1993 season were overshadowed by the sudden loss of two of NASCAR's brightest stars. Alan Kulwicki had achieved success in Winston Cup racing in his own fashion, with his own team. As an independent owner, the odds were against him, yet, despite the naysayers and the lucrative offers from other owners eager to add his talents to their teams, he stuck to his guns and fulfilled his dream. The 1992 champion didn't have long to enjoy his accomplishment: on April 1, the small plane in which Kulwicki was flying with executives from sponsor Hooters Restaurants crashed en route to Bristol. The race world was stunned by the news. Kulwicki was an intensely private man, but universally admired, a genuine representative of the best qualities of the sport.

Before the NASCAR community could catch its breath after the loss of its reigning champion, tragedy struck again. Davey Allison had flown his helicopter to Talladega to watch David Bonnett (Neil's son) run test laps. As he hovered over the landing pad, the chopper suddenly flipped over and crashed. Red Farmer, flying with Allison, escaped the wreckage, but Allison was critically injured. The Allison clan was still reeling from loss of Davey's younger brother, Clifford, in a racing accident.

When Davey died days later, they were devastated. The NASCAR family had lost another favorite son.

Ernie Irvan, eventually named Allison's successor in the #28, brought the team two wins in that first season. Hooters withdrew their sponsorship from the #7 team, which was sold to Geoffrey Bodine.

Though the season was marred by these tragic losses, it had its bright spots. A new track was added to the schedule—Bob Bahre's gorgeous New Hampshire facility. The outstanding Rookie of the Year class included Kenny Wallace, Bobby Labonte, and a young fellow who'd recently moved up to the Busch Grand National ranks from racing sprints—Jeff Gordon. Gordon formed a third team with Rick Hendrick and crew chief Ray Evernham, in what turned out to be a perfect combination. When Gordon won his first race, a Daytona Twin 125, at the start of the year, he was the first rookie to do so since

---

Jeff Gordon shortens the back end of the #24 car. Gordon has reached the level of success where, paradoxically, fans begin to boo him for winning and cheer when he wrecks or breaks down. With few exceptions, drivers who have dominated the circuit for a period of years—Waltrip, Wallace, Earnhardt—have gone through this.

1963. The team had an up-and-down season as they learned the ropes, scoring seven top-fives and suffering a number of crashes as Gordon adjusted to the heavier cars and new tracks. He was a quick study, though, and would put those lessons to good use the next year. The March race at Atlanta was delayed, but not by rain—the Blizzard of the Century had buried Atlanta under inches of snow.

Rick Wilson drove the STP car in Petty's first season behind the pit wall. Popular sentiment convinced Petty to retire the #43 at the end of his driving career and, at least for this year, the car was renumbered #44.

Dale Jarrett and the Joe Gibbs #18 team had a great sophomore year. The "Dale and Dale" show at Daytona saw Jarrett win the Daytona 500, leading Dale Earnhardt to the finish as Dale's father, Ned, excitedly coached him through the last lap from the TV broadcast booth. That win and twelve top-fives were enough to place Jarrett fourth in the standings. Mark Martin became the latest driver to run off four consecutive wins, from Watkins Glen through the Southern 500. With a fifth win later in the season he earned third-place standing at the end.

ABOVE: *Rusty Wallace's #2 Pontiac becomes airborne at Talladega in the 1993 Winston 500. In the jostling on the last lap of a two-lap shootout, Wallace and Earnhardt touched and Wallace's Pontiac started a series of barrel rolls, carrying him across the finish line for a top-ten finish.* LEFT: *Last-minute checks on Mark Martin's Busch Grand National car. Many of the Winston Cup drivers drive in the Grand National races when the two series are at the same track for a weekend.*

The battle for the championship was fought mostly between Earnhardt and Rusty Wallace. Earnhardt again took the early lead, but Wallace put together four wins in eight races and pulled ahead. Wallace's hot streak cooled somewhat after the Winston 500. A tap from Earnhardt on the last lap sent Rusty's #2 tumbling down the front stretch. Amazingly, he flew over the finish line for sixth place. Wallace wasn't seriously injured, but the accident took him out of his game; with four straight DNFs due to mechanical failures, he wound up far behind Earnhardt in the points standings. Wallace made a late-season charge with three more wins, but Earnhardt countered with a string of top-fives. Wallace fell short by eighty points. Not to minimize Earnhardt's season—he had won six races on his way to this sixth championship—but the outcome brought the points scheme under fire again. How could a team win ten races, a full third of the schedule, as Wallace had done, and still lose the title?

Both Dale and Rusty paid tribute to their absent friends. The Bristol audience was hushed as Wallace saluted Alan Kulwicki with a "Polish victory lap" after Wallace's win there. After a victory in Pocono, Dale Earnhardt remembered both Kulwicki and Davey Allison as the RCR crew gathered at the start-finish line for a prayer.

The 1993 season also saw a pack of stock cars running at the legendary Indianapolis Motorspeedway for the first time. Tire tests had been done the previous year and, following the outcomes of the driver tests, a race date was planned for 1994. More than thirty drivers took to the Brickyard, running speeds of about 165 mph (266kph). Reaction to the news was mixed. The Indy Car drivers were skeptical, but the fans were receptive, finding the NASCAR drivers accessible and the action close.

ABOVE: *Jeff Gordon's first win, at the 1994 Coca-Cola 600 in Charlotte. Gordon's wasn't the fastest car on the track, but pit strategy put him at the front for the win.*
OPPOSITE: *Jack Rousch added a second car to his team in 1992. Ted Musgrave came on board in 1994 in the Family Channel #16 car.*

1993 Championship Standings

Place	Car#	Driver	Car Type	Points
1	3	Dale Earnhardt	Chevy	4,526
2	2	Rusty Wallace	Pontiac	4,446
3	6	Mark Martin	Ford	4,150
4	18	Dale Jarrett	Chevy	4,000
5	42	Kyle Petty	Pontiac	3,860
6	4/28	Ernie Irvan	Chevy/Ford	3,834
7	21	Morgan Shepherd	Ford	3,807
8	11	Bill Elliott	Ford	3,774
9	25	Ken Schrader	Chevy	3,715
10	5	Ricky Rudd	Chevy	3,644

1994: Earnhardt Ties Petty and the Bandit Hangs Up His Helmet

Neil Bonnett had been away from driving since his injury in a racing accident in 1990. In 1993, after being given the medical go-ahead, he ran two events and was all set to run a limited schedule in 1994, including the Daytona 500. A longtime friend of many in NASCAR and a fan favorite, Bonnett had remained involved during his convalescence (through broadcasting) and was eager to resume racing. In a nightmarish continuation of 1993, however, Bonnett cut a tire during a practice session, turned head-on into the front-stretch wall, and was killed by the impact.

Hoosier Tires, which had made a run at the Winston Cup in 1988, was back in the picture in 1994. A number of teams saw an advantage to the Hoosier formula: Geoffrey Bodine won seven poles and three races on Hoosiers, an outstanding performance in his first year as a car owner. As in 1988, though, concerns over safety in the resulting "tire war" prevailed and Hoosier withdrew.

Another old-timer announced his retirement that year. Harry Gant, who'd raced in the Winston Cup since the mid-1970s, let it be known that 1994 would be his last year. Like Cale Yarborough, Gant cited the best of all

reasons—he wanted to spend more time with his family. The 1994 season was dubbed "the Bandit's Last Ride," and Leo Jackson honored Gant with a special paint scheme at his final race in Atlanta, duplicating the colors of Gant's first Skoal Bandit car in 1981.

Junior Johnson looked to turn up the heat on his second team, replacing Hut Stricklin in the McDonald's #27 with "Mr. Excitement," Jimmy Spencer. Spencer came through, earning wins at Daytona and Talladega. Richard Petty let Rick Wilson go after a dismal season. Wally Dallenbach Jr. started the season in the #43 (returning Petty's signature number to the active roster) but was replaced by John Andretti. Rick Rudd was the latest driver to form his own team, retaining Tide sponsorship for his #10 Fords, and extending his winning streak with a victory in New Hampshire. When, after several lackluster years, Terry Labonte left Billy Hagan's team to take the Hendrick #5 ride, the move rejuvenated his career. Winless since his stint with Junior Johnson, Labonte scored three victories in 1994, the most he'd ever won in a season.

Jeff Gordon's #24 team lived up to its potential in its second season, and the young driver let his emotion show in victory lane when he won his first race, at the Coca-Cola 600 in Charlotte. Gordon got his second win that year, also, in the inaugural Brickyard 400, taking the lead from Ernie Irvan when the #28 cut a tire at the end of the race. Although the team had yet to find consistency, its seven top-fives were enough for eighth place in the points standings.

The 1994 Daytona 500 was characterized by firsts. Loy Allen Jr., a contender for Rookie of the Year, was the first rookie ever to win a Daytona pole. Sterling Marlin got his first victory, in his first race with the #4 Kodak team. Observers noted during practice runs that Marlin's car had a different sound, more like an Indy car than a stock car. Whatever engine builder Runt Pittman had done, he'd done it right—Marlin ran strong all day.

With the win at Daytona and a second at Rockingham, Marlin took the early points lead, but Ernie Irvan won the next two races in a row and took over at the top. Earnhardt responded with two wins of his own and passed Irvan. A couple of races later, Irvan was back on top. The two continued swapping the lead through the first half of the season, together pulling away from third-place Rusty Wallace. Wallace's team had switched from Pontiac to Ford in 1994 and, although they could win races, they were not consistent finishers and trailed the leaders by three hundred points going into the autumn.

The complexion of the season altered completely at the second Michigan race. It was Earnhardt's turn at the top, and he held a slim lead over Irvan. While running practice

1994 Championship Standings

Place	Car#	Driver	Car Type	Points
1	3	Dale Earnhardt	Chevy	4,694
2	6	Mark Martin	Ford	4,250
3	2	Rusty Wallace	Ford	4,207
4	25	Ken Schrader	Chevy	4,060
5	10	Ricky Rudd	Ford	4,050
6	21	Morgan Shepherd	Ford	4,029
7	5	Terry Labonte	Chevy	3,876
8	24	Jeff Gordon	Chevy	3,776
9	17	Darrell Waltrip	Chevy	3,688
10	11	Bill Elliott	Ford	3,617

One facet of Winston Cup racing that fans often take for granted is the television coverage. ESPN, TNN, TBS, CBS, and ABC all currently televise races and have crews of professional broadcasters and knowledgeable analysts to call the events. One of the best announcers is Ned Jarrett, former Grand National champion (and father of current competitor Dale Jarrett).

Winston Cup racing has attracted talent from many walks of life. The #18 team is fielded by the former coach of the Washington Redskins, Joe Gibbs. Gibbs' talent for selecting top-notch people and his strong leadership have brought the team to championship contention after only a few years on the circuit. Bobby Labonte, with seven wins to date, was joined by a second Gibbs team in 1999, featuring open-wheel racer Tony Stewart in the #20 car. Both cars finnished near the top of the points standings that year.

laps, Irvan lost a tire and went hard into the wall; rescue workers found him unconscious. He was evacuated to a local hospital, and friends and family held their breath over the next few days. Irvan's a fighter, and he pulled through the danger zone and began a long convalescence.

With Irvan out of the race, Earnhardt had the championship run to himself. Wallace made another late-season charge, but Earnhardt was looking for a place in history that year and would have none of it. With every Wallace win (eight in all), Earnhardt finished right behind him, giving up very little of his lead.

Dale Earnhardt had done what had barely seemed possible, tying Richard Petty's remarkable record of seven championships—and all in the ultracompetitive modern era.

1995: Gordon Takes His Place at the Podium

The Winston Cup turned twenty-five in 1995, celebrating its silver anniversary. Chevy introduced a new—or rather an old—model to replace the Lumina that year. The Monte Carlo was back, and stronger than ever: Chevys swept the first seven races of the season and won thirteen of the first sixteen. The car was so dominant that NASCAR took to impounding one of each make after selected races to analyze them in comparative wind-tunnel testing.

The 1995 silly season was exceptionally silly, with almost half of the teams sporting new drivers or crew chiefs. With Ernie Irvan unable to compete at the beginning of the season, Robert Yates was looking for a new driver for the second straight year. Dale Jarrett got the nod and left the #18 team to wear Texaco colors. The strength of the #28 car and team had been proven, first with Davey Allison then with Irvan, so the pressure was on Jarrett to live up to the ride. The team didn't come together right away, but Jarrett eventually won one race, late in the season. To everyone's amazement, Ernie Irvan was back in a driver's uniform near the end of 1995. He had resumed

racing in the Craftsman Truck series to get back on his feet, and returned to Winston Cup at Martinsville in a second Yates car (#88, in memory of Roberts' old days at DiGard). He ran three races in 1995, snatching two top-tens, putting to rest any questions about his desire and ability to drive.

Michael Kranefuss from Ford and Carl Haas of Indy Car fame joined forces to form a NASCAR team. The #37 had Kmart and Little Caesar's as sponsors and Indy car regular John Andretti as driver. John was the second Andretti, following uncle Mario, to try his hand at NASCAR.

Bobby Labonte moved to Joe Gibbs' #18 team, replacing Dale Jarrett, and immediately took off—the team won both Michigan races and the Coca-Cola 600 at Charlotte in its first season. Clearly, Terry was not the only talented Labonte brother. Ward Burton was another first-time winner that year; his #22 was clearly the strongest car in the autumn Rockingham race, although a late-race caution put his lead in jeopardy. During a pit stop, officials thought that Earnhardt had exited with a lug nut missing. They black-flagged him but found when he entered the pits that all the nuts were on and secure. Meanwhile, Dale went down a lap. Seeking to correct the situation, NASCAR threw an unprecedented caution flag and allowed Earnhardt to go around the track and take up his previous lead lap position. Well and good for the #3, but Ward Burton's solid lead was suddenly a little shakier, and Rusty Wallace was sitting right on his tail for the restart. Again NASCAR took action, interposing lapped cars between Burton and second-place Wallace to allow Ward a reasonable advantage on the start. Burton hung on and captured his first win.

The Rookie of the Year battle was fought between Robert Pressley, Harry Gant's replacement in the new Skoal #33, and Ricky Craven. The competition was close, but it was Craven who came out on top.

Initially, 1995 looked like a repeat of 1994. Sterling Marlin won his second consecutive Daytona 500 but ceded the points lead to Earnhardt several races later. This year, though, there was a joker in the pack. Jeff Gordon and the #24 team had finally gelled, winning two races early on.

Sterling Marlin finishes a strong second in the Napa 500 season-closer at Atlanta in 1995. His performance moved him into third in points for the year, his best rank ever. Marlin had gone seventeen years in Winston Cup without winning a race, but in his first three years with the Kodak team he scored six wins.

Folks in the garage were beginning to wonder if the young team might post a challenge to the old hands at RCR.

Gordon moved up in the points standings quickly, from twenty-first to tying for the lead with Earnhardt going into the Sears Point race in May. Earnhardt filled in one of the few blank spots on his résumé there, winning his first road course race by slipping past Mark Martin with two laps to go. Earnhardt maintained the points lead until the June Michigan race, when a thirty-fifth-place finish allowed Sterling Marlin to move past him by six points. Gordon was right behind them in third place, only six points behind Dale. The three teams remained in a deadlock for several weeks. Gordon finally broke loose with two more wins, at Daytona and New Hampshire, and two second-place finishes. Earnhardt managed three more wins in the second half of the year, including the second running of the Brickyard 400, but continued to fall behind Gordon. By autumn, Gordon had a three-

ABOVE: *Terry Labonte started second in the 1995 TransSouth 500 at Darlington, but was caught up in a crash that brought out one of the record-setting fifteen yellow flags on the day.*
OPPOSITE TOP: *The Kodak #4 team watches the race from pit wall, and with good reason. After a series of crashes, the race had become a showdown between their car and Earnhardt's Goodwrench #3. With twelve laps left, though, Sterling Marlin took the lead for good and won the race. Many teams now have TV monitors built into their pit boxes to allow them to watch the action all around the track.*
OPPOSITE BOTTOM: *Bill Elliott settles into "racing mode." Many drivers say that they are the most relaxed when they're finally strapped down in the car.*

The Silly Season

It happens in every sport: owners improve their teams by raiding talent from other teams. In the early days of NASCAR, drivers and owners rarely had any sort of long-term contract binding them. They'd stick together as long as the team was productive and the chemistry was good. Only in the 1970s did observers start to see drivers entering into multiyear contracts. Darrell Waltrip was one of the first—and most interesting—examples. When the relationship didn't work out, the DiGard team had to come to terms with the realization that to be truly competitive in Winston Cup racing, you needed more than just a legal arrangement.

As NASCAR became more competitive—and sponsors increasingly demanded results to justify their investments—teams constantly searched for that perfect combination of owner, crew chief, and driver. When the chemistry wasn't right, or the team couldn't produce top finishes quickly, personnel changes usually followed. At the level of commitment required in Winston Cup racing, owners and sponsors are rarely willing to take chances on new, untested talent. This means that there is a limited pool of drivers and crew chiefs available to teams, so anytime a crew chief or driver leaves a ride or is relieved, it triggers a widespread personnel shuffle. Drivers who are unsatisfied with their teams look to improve their situations by jumping to a better ride, just as owners go after better drivers or look to fill vacancies. This ritual, which usually begins in late summer or early fall, as teams try to firm up plans and sponsorship money for the next year, has come to be known as "the silly season."

In some years, the cycle is intense and widespread. A typical—and typically perplexing—silly season was 1996. It went a little like this:

Ken Schrader, who had not had a good season with the Hendrick #25 team for years, decided it was time to try another ride. Andy Petree, who had taken over the #33 team from Leo Jackson, didn't feel he had the time to wait for his driver, Robert Pressley, to mature, so he offered Schrader the Skoal ride. Schrader moved from #25 to #33. Pressley was out of a ride.

Ricky Craven, seeing the opportunity of a lifetime, jumped out of partnership in the #41 team to move to Hendrick's stable in the #25. So now the #41 was open. Gary Bechtold, owner of the #29 team, was dissatisfied with Steve

Ward Burton leads on the way to his first win, at the 1995 ACDelco 400 at Rockingham. Burton had a substantial lead over Rusty Wallace when NASCAR threw a yellow flag to allow Earnhardt to make up a lap he was improperly penalized. On the restart NASCAR allowed Burton to line up with lapped cars between him and Wallace to maintain his previous advantage. He held on and took the checkered.

Grissom and released him. Grissom hooked up with Larry Hedrick and took the #41 ride. Bechtold, with an open car, took Pressley.

In an unusual move, John Andretti and Jeremy Mayfield swapped rides, with Mayfield moving from the #98 to the #37, and vice versa for Andretti. Same deal for the #1 and #75 cars: Rick Mast went from #1 to #75, Morgan Shepherd went from #75 to #1.

Now, each year some teams go away and some new teams start up. The #12 Bobby Allison team shut down after 1996, leaving Derrike Cope high and dry. He picked up a new ride with the #36 team. Joe Falk started a new #91 team, grabbing Mike Wallace as the driver from the #90 Donlavey crew. Dick Trickle, who'd had various fill-in roles in 1996, became the full-time #90 driver. Kyle Petty and Felix Sabates split up. Petty started a new #44 team at RPE, Sabates filled the #42 with Joe Nemecheck, who had sold his #87 team to Sabates (whereupon the number changed to #42). Bud Moore's fabled #15 team closed shop after 1996, releasing Wally Dallenbach. Luckily, Sabates started another new team and Dallenbach moved to the #46.

The only new drivers to enter the mix in 1997 were Indy car racer Robby Gordon (whom Sabates brought on in another new team) and truck racer Mike Skinner (whom Richard Childress brought on in a new team). Greg Sacks had a ride for the start of the season in the new #20 team but lost the sponsorship and the ride after a handful of races.

Who's the winner once the dust settles? The merchandise peddlers, of course. With each shift of personnel, the merchandisers have an entirely new set of T-shirt designs, collectible toy cars, and other paraphernalia they can bring to market the following year.

The owner of the #41, Larry Hedrick is still in search of the formula to take him to the winner's circle. He thought he had it in 1995 with rookie driver Ricky Craven. Craven had a promising Busch Grand National career and showed commitment when he bought into the team as part-owner. But he moved to Rick Hendrick's #25 team when that ride opened up in 1997.

hundred-point lead over the seven-time champ. As many had expected, however, the pressure of the title race started to weigh on the inexperienced team. Earnhardt chewed away at the lead, reducing it to fewer than 150 points going into the season finale. Dale did everything he could in that last race, leading the most laps and winning the event. Gordon helped out quite a bit as well, finishing a dismal thirty-second. The lead had shrunk to thirty-four points, but that was still enough to block Earnhardt from winning a historic eighth title and to give the youngster—the second-youngest champion in NASCAR history, and the youngest in the modern era—his first title.

1995 Championship Standings

Place	Car#	Driver	Car Type	Points
1	24	Jeff Gordon	Chevy	4,614
2	3	Dale Earnhardt	Chevy	4,580
3	4	Sterling Marlin	Chevy	4,361
4	6	Mark Martin	Ford	4,320
5	2	Rusty Wallace	Ford	4,240
6	5	Terry Labonte	Chevy	4,146
7	16	Ted Musgrave	Ford	3,949
8	94	Bill Elliott	Ford	3,746
9	10	Ricky Rudd	Ford	3,734
10	18	Bobby Labonte	Pontiac	3,718

It was mathematically possible—if Gordon finished dead last at Atlanta, and Earnhardt won and led the most laps, Dale could have caught Gordon for the 1995 championship. Earnhardt held up his end of the deal, dominating the race and taking the win. Gordon wouldn't comply, though—his thirty-second-place finish was good enough to take the title. Here, Gordon celebrates his first championship in the infield.

1996: Labonte Wins His Second after Twelve Years

One of the big stories in 1996 was the competitiveness of qualifying. It used to be that qualifying was almost perfunctory: all of the regulars got starting positions. As NASCAR's popularity skyrocketed, however, more and more teams were interested in running Winston Cup races, many with solid financial backing and fast cars. Series regulars suddenly found themselves struggling to make races. A number of top teams—including the #28, #42, and #94—had to use provisional spots through the season just to get in the field. Provisionals are sort of "pass go" cards that teams can use to offset poor qualifying runs. Each field has a number of designated provisional spaces at the back, which are assigned to teams as needed, with teams higher in the standings getting priority. Each team starts the year with four provisional slots and earns an additional one for every eight qualifying attempts.

This was the year that saw the end of one of NASCAR's longest and most successful associations. Junior Johnson sold his #27 team to Hooters CEO Bob Brooks, and the fabled #11 team to Brett Bodine, who'd driven for him in that car the previous year. Johnson had been involved with NASCAR since 1953 and had been a team owner since 1966. Another sad loss was the death of master mechanic Harry Hyde, who suffered a heart attack in May.

Michael Waltrip and Chuck Rider split up the Bahari team after nine years together. Waltrip moved to the Wood Brothers #21 and Morgan Shepherd left that ride for Butch Mock's #75 Ford. One of the more interesting new sponsorships was on the Melling #9 car driven by Lake Speed. The bright blue-and-yellow car, featuring a well-known

processed lunch meat, was popularly referred to as the "Spam Can." And after Indy Car driver Robby Gordon tried his hand at NASCAR in a one-race run at Charlotte, he and Felix Sabates signed a deal to run full-schedule in 1997.

Ernie Irvan was back full-time in the #28 ride in 1996, but Robert Yates wanted to retain Dale Jarrett as well, so he formed a second team. Jarrett moved to the #88 with Ford Credit as sponsor and Todd Parrott (son of veteran Buddy Parrott) as crew chief. The team clicked right away and put together five wins in its freshman year—including a run at the Winston Million. Jarrett won the Daytona 500 (his second) and the Coca-Cola 600 and was leading the Southern 500 comfortably when he hit a patch of oil and smacked into the wall. Jarrett joined Darrell Waltrip and Davey Allison in the small circle of "almost" winners of the grand prize. Irvan also won

This is not the view you want to have at the start of a race. Darrell Waltrip and Dave Marcis start scratch in the Miller 500 at Dover in 1996. They finished near the back as well, while pole-sitter Jeff Gordon got his third win of the year.

two races in 1996. His New Hampshire win was the first since his accident and was an emotional moment for the team. His season was uneven, though, and he finished tenth in points.

Sterling Marlin continued his dominance of restrictor-plate tracks with wins at Talladega and in the summer Daytona race. Talladega lived up to its reputation for drama again this year. In the first race, a high-speed crash catapulted Ricky Craven's car into the air, across the track, and over other cars. Craven suffered only minor injuries, but Bill Elliott, in a separate incident, ended up with a broken leg when his car lifted into the air, then slammed back down. Elliott was unable to race for several weeks as a result. The July Daytona race also saw Earnhardt in a crash that resulted in broken bones. There was drama before the race as well, when NASCAR selected pole winner Irvan's car to test their new dynamometer. The NASCAR inspectors accidentally over-revved the engine during the test, ruining it for the race. Needless to say, the #28 team was less than happy.

Ricky Rudd kept his streak going with a win at the end of the season at Rockingham. Bobby Hamilton, in Richard Petty's #43, was a first-time winner at Phoenix,

Petty Enterprises finally broke a long winless stretch in 1996, when Bobby Hamilton took the #43 to victory lane with a win at Phoenix Raceway. One year to the day later, Hamilton again piloted the STP Pontiac to a win at the fall race in Rockingham.

putting the King's car back in victory lane for the first time since 1984. Petty missed the winner's circle in a different race, though, when he ran for North Carolina secretary of state and was defeated despite his widespread popularity.

Rusty Wallace put together another winning season, with five victories, but was unable to keep up with the series leaders and finished the season seventh in points. Rusty did have the distinction of winning NASCAR's first international race, when a number of NASCAR teams joined local drivers at the Suzuka road course for a post-season exhibition race. It was a non-points event, but was very well received by the fans in Japan—and it gave the drivers of NASCAR a chance to broaden their horizons.

Johnny Benson Jr. moved up from his Busch Grand National championship to win Rookie of the Year in the Bahari #30 car.

Earnhardt's championship express train, temporarily derailed in 1995, seemed to be back on track at the beginning of the 1996 season. Despite not winning the Daytona 500 again (and becoming understandably testy when reporters continued to ask him when he would win it), he was at the top of the standings again in the first part of the season, aided by wins at Rockingham and Atlanta. Hendrick's gang had its own ideas about the points lead,

1996 Championship Standings

Place	Car#	Driver	Car Type	Points
1	5	Terry Labonte	Chevy	4,657
2	24	Jeff Gordon	Chevy	4,620
3	88	Dale Jarrett	Ford	4,568
4	3	Dale Earnhardt	Chevy	4,327
5	6	Mark Martin	Ford	4,278
6	10	Ricky Rudd	Ford	3,845
7	2	Rusty Wallace	Ford	3,717
8	4	Sterling Marlin	Chevy	3,682
9	43	Bobby Hamilton	Pontiac	3,639
10	28	Ernie Irvan	Ford	3,632

however, and began closing in. They did it in different ways: Jeff Gordon showed flashes of brilliance, winning at Richmond, Bristol, Darlington, Dover, and Pocono; Terry Labonte picked up only one win in the first half of the season, at North Wilkesboro, but doggedly accumulated one top-five after another, and by midsummer was on top of the points. Going into the August Michigan race, Gordon and Earnhardt were tied for second place, with Dale Jarrett only three points back in fourth.

Going into the autumn, the bottom fell out for Earnhardt. At Talladega in July he was caught up in a severe crash that left him with a broken collarbone and sternum. He showed the world that he was still "One Tough Customer" by starting the next race at Indy despite his injuries, but went into a downspin in September. Other than a sixth-place finish at the Glen, he had eight consecutive midpack finishes, which dropped him to fourth in points, behind Labonte, Gordon, and Jarrett. Gordon continued to add trophies to his case (he would garner ten in all for the year) but Labonte won at Charlotte and—with top-fives at Rockingham, Phoenix, and Atlanta—maintained a thirty-seven-point advantage over his teammate to win the championship.

This was a special year for Labonte, who won his second championship after a twelve-year drought. He also added the title "Ironman" to his résumé when he passed Richard Petty's long-standing record of 513 consecutive starts. The season ended fittingly when brother Bobby won the Atlanta race and the Labontes circled the track together, both of them victors.

OPPOSITE TOP: *Father and son finish one-two for the first time since 1960. "It was a great feeling at the finish to look back and see somebody you think is the best coming up in the sport and know it's your son," Bobby Allison said of Davey's second-place finish.*
OPPOSITE BOTTOM: *Brothers Terry and Bobby Labonte run together in the 1996 ACDelco 400. Both are top performers and it's not uncommon to see them vying for position together near the front of the field in any race.*

NASCAR Families

When people talk about the NASCAR family, they often mean more than the fraternity and sorority of drivers, crewmembers, and employees. More so than almost any other sport, stock car racing is a fellowship of brothers, fathers, sons, and grandsons, husbands, wives, and in-laws. As a result, the extended NASCAR "family" is a close-knit group. The people are on good terms, even among competing teams (usually), and they look out for one another. Unlike in the "elite" motorsports series, it's not uncommon for a driver to jump out of a car to help a fellow driver in trouble, or for crewmembers to lend a hand to the team in the pit stall next door.

Some of the most dramatic moments in NASCAR history have been those shared by father and son or by brothers: Bobby Allison rushing to his son's aid when the two crashed at Darlington in 1987 and Davey's car burst into flames; Bobby and Davey sharing first and second place in victory lane at Daytona; Bobby defending brother Donnie from an enraged Cale Yarborough after the famous 1979 Daytona crash. Another memorable moment came at the end of the 1996 season, when Bobby Labonte won the final race at Atlanta and brother Terry wrapped up the championship. The two winners circled the track together, to a standing ovation.

Although Dale Jarrett never had the opportunity to race with his father, two-time champion Ned, they were able to share some of Dale's victories by virtue of Ned's position as television broadcaster. Viewers were treated to Ned's emotional calling of his son's 1993 Daytona 500 win, as dad talked his son through the last lap to victory over Dale Earnhardt.

Lee and Richard Petty, and Ned and Dale Jarrett have the distinction of being the only multigenerational champions. The Pettys are also the only three-generation family in NASCAR, although the Earnhardts are on the verge of joining that club with Dale Jr. following Ralph and Dale Sr.'s lead.

Other father-son combos include Buck and Buddy Baker, David and Larry Pearson, and Clifton "Coo Coo" and Sterling Marlin. NASCAR's brother teams are almost too numerous to mention. There haven't yet been any sibling champions, but Ken and Ron Bouchard share the distinction of both having been Rookies of the Year. The Flocks, Wallaces, and Bodines are all three-brother racing families. The Flocks are unique in that for at least part of a season they were joined on the circuit by their sister, Ethel Flock Mobley. Among the brother acts, Bobby and Donnie Allison share the most wins, ninety-five, with the Flocks (Fonty, Tim, and Bob) next in line with sixty-two. Among active sibling drivers at this writing, Terry and Bobby Labonte have the most combined wins. Other families with more than one winner include those of Herb and Don Thomas, Geoffrey and Brett Bodine, Jeff and Ward Burton, and Benny and Phil Parsons.

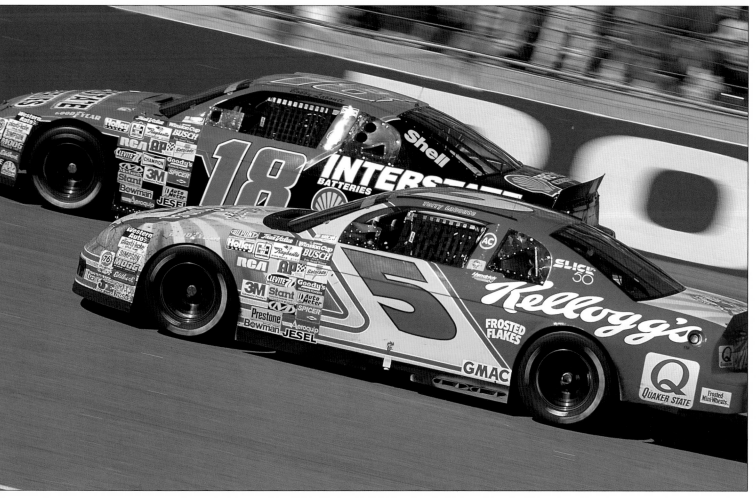

1997: No "Flash," Gordon Earns His Second Title

In 1997, Darrell Waltrip celebrated his twenty-fifth year in NASCAR. His #17 cars were painted with different schemes representing his various rides through the years, with a special chrome car to boot. Waltrip had had his last win in 1992, and he'd been struggling over the last few years. Despite rumors to the contrary, and his first DNQ ("did not qualify") at Charlotte, he made it clear that he wasn't ready to retire. "Given equal equipment on any given Sunday," he said, "I think I'm as good as any driver." By year's end, D.W. would improve on his 1996 season with a top-five and four top-tens.

Rusty Wallace was raring for a championship in 1997. He had a new color scheme on his Miller Lite Fords and was confident that this would be his season. Rusty had the right attitude, but the the team wasn't there to back it up. Wallace won only once, and with twelve top-tens finished ninth in the points. Ernie Irvan got back on the horse that threw him, winning at the Michigan track where he'd been critically injured in 1994. His season was up and down, though, and worried sponsors led Robert Yates to announce that in 1998 he would replace Ernie with rookie Kenny Irwin, who got a sneak preview of Winston Cup

action in several 1997 races. Irwin showed why he'd been selected by putting his #27 car on the outside pole at Richmond and finishing eighth.

Ricky Rudd extended his streak to sixteen winning seasons (tying Earnhardt) with wins at the Brickyard and at Dover. He inherited the Dover victory in a strange race that saw the three previous leaders wreck. John Andretti, who had moved to the Cale Yarborough team in 1997, scored his first Winston Cup win (Cale's first as an owner) at the July Daytona race. Kyle Petty left Felix Sabates' team to form a second Petty team ("PE2") with #44 and Hot Wheels (a fitting sponsor) on the car.

Two new tracks were added to the schedule for 1997 and one was dropped. Bob Bahre and O. Bruton Smith shared ownership of the North Wilkesboro track, but Bahre also owned New Hampshire, and Smith a new track in Texas. In order to expand the New Hampshire facility to two races, and for Smith to get a date in Texas, they closed down the Wilkesboro facility and took the open dates. The Texas Speedway race was fraught with wrecks: ten caution flags flew. Many drivers, Rusty Wallace the most outspoken of them, felt the track was too narrow to race competitively and would require major work. By contrast, Roger Penske's new California Speedway, added to

the schedule in May (now at thirty-two races), was a jewel. Jeff Burton was the inaugural Texas race winner, while Jeff Gordon took California.

Terry Labonte, who had won the previous year's title on consistency—only two wins but countless top-fives—was unable to repeat that performance to defend his title in 1997. Terry started the year off well and held the points lead in the spring, but with only one win and eight top-fives during the year he ended up dropping to sixth in the standings. Though paired with ace crew chief Larry McReynolds—who'd been lured from the #28 team—Dale Earnhardt continued a winless streak that had started after the first Atlanta race the previous year, and he was never a contender for the championship. Besides logging his first winless season since 1981, Earnhardt suffered a mysterious blackout in the Southern 500 that left folks questioning his ability to race. When doctors were unable to find anything amiss, Earnhardt got the green light to resume. He finished fifth in the points standings.

Jeff Burton was the surprise contender in 1997. With his first three wins, in Jack Rousch's #99, Burton pulled up to fourth in the points standings. The battle for the title, however, was waged among Jeff Gordon, Mark Martin, and Dale Jarrett. Gordon started it off at Daytona with his

OPPOSITE: *Teams keep extensive notebooks on car setups at each track. These include crib notes on what other teams are doing as well as what they've done on their own. These notes provide invaluable insight into the inner workings of a Winston Cup team.* ABOVE: *Owner Harry Melling retained the #9 after Bill Elliott left in 1992, employing a string of drivers over the intervening years. Jerry Nadeau currently pilots the Cartoon Network entry, seen here at the ACDelco 400 at Rockingham.*

1997 Championship Standings

Place	Car#	Driver	Car Type	Points
1	24	Jeff Gordon	Chevy	4,710
2	88	Dale Jarrett	Ford	4,696
3	6	Mark Martin	Ford	4,681
4	99	Jeff Burton	Ford	4,285
5	3	Dale Earnhardt	Chevy	4,216
6	5	Terry Labonte	Chevy	4,177
7	18	Bobby Labonte	Pontiac	4,101
8	94	Bill Elliott	Ford	3,836
9	2	Rusty Wallace	Ford	3,598
10	33	Ken Schrader	Chevy	3,576

first 500 win there. The winner's circle was a Rick Hendrick photo op, as teammates Labonte and Ricky Craven (replacing Ken Schrader, the new Skoal Bandit) finished second and third, respectively. By the Michigan race in June, Gordon had won six out of fourteen races and was still in the points lead. Jeff found himself one of an elite group of drivers who over the years have been booed by fans for winning too often for the onlookers' frequently egalitarian tastes.

Mark Martin briefly wrested the lead from Gordon with wins at Michigan and at Bristol (combined with Gordon's thirty-fifth-place finish at the latter), but Gordon reclaimed it the next week with his third straight Southern 500 win—a new record. The Darlington win was special for another reason as well. Gordon had won at Daytona and he'd won the Coca-Cola 600. The Southern 500 was the last qualifying race for the Winston Million; Jeff joined Bill Elliott as only the second driver to collect that purse. Any doubt about Gordon's desire and ability to win was put to rest as he stubbornly held off a determined Jeff Burton at the end of race.

Gordon and his Rainbow Warrior crew had been awesome all year, but they fell prey to an autumn slump. Going into the September Martinsville race, Gordon had a 165-point lead over second-place Mark Martin. He saw that lead slip away over the last few races of the season, as he suffered a thirty-fifth-place finish at Talladega and a seventeenth in Phoenix. Going into Atlanta his lead had shrunk to seventy-seven points over Jarrett and eighty-seven over Martin.

The Atlanta weekend didn't begin auspiciously for Gordon. The configuration of the track had been changed since the spring race, so everyone was back to square one. On top of that, rain forced cancellation of Friday's qualifying session. There would only be one brief practice on Saturday and a single qualifying session. It looked like Gordon's luck had completely run out when he lost control of his car as he pulled into pit row during practice and slammed into the back of the parked #43. Both teams frantically began work on backup cars, but time was short and Gordon was only able to qualify in thirty-seventh place. Jarrett started third, Martin ninth. Gordon struggled all day to move up through the field in the ill-handling car. As Bobby Labonte won his second straight season finale, Gordon managed only a seventeenth-place finish. Jarrett and Martin finished second and third, respectively. The points lead had shrunk to fourteen, but Gordon was still on top.

Mike Skinner won Rookie of the Year honors in a second Richard Childress car.

1998: NASCAR Turns Fifty

In the years since R.J. Reynolds had instituted the Winston Million, only two drivers, Bill Elliott in 1985 and Jeff Gordon in 1997, had won the full award. In 1998, RJR announced a significant update: instead of $1 million, the new "No Bull 5" program would be worth $5 million, and would involve five races—the four traditional events plus the Brickyard 400. The top five finishers in each of those events would be eligible for $1 million if they won the next of the five races, and so on, with eligibility carrying over from the end of one year to the next. Not only did this change quintuple the purse, but that purse was infinitely more attainable than the Winston Million. And many more drivers had a shot at the award over the course of a season. As Elliott had in the first year of the Winston Million, the Winston Cup aces immediately demonstrated that they were capable of winning this award.

The Winston Cup schedule continued to expand, with Las Vegas Speedway added to the circuit. Bobby Hamilton left the STP shop for the #4 Kodak ride, while John Andretti rejoined Petty in the #43. Sterling Marlin went to the Felix Sabates #40 team, replacing the volatile and accident-prone Robby Gordon (Sabates kept a pair of boxing gloves in his office for his meetings with Gordon). Roger Penske came on as part owner of the Michael Kranefuss #37 team. The operation changed to #12 (an old Penske favorite), acquired Mobil 1 as a sponsor, and retained Jeremy Mayfield as driver. With Penske's involvement, Mayfield and Rusty Wallace became teammates, and their matching blue-and-white Fords ran together near the front for much of the season. Jack Rousch continued expanding his operation, adding the team of Chad Little and forming a new team for Johnny Benson Jr. Rousch Racing fielded five cars full-time in the 1998 season and saw two of them regularly visit the winner's circle.

Darrell Waltrip was once again on the verge of retirement, this time due to sponsor troubles. When his sponsor, Speedblock, pulled out, leaving Waltrip stranded, he put his #17 team into hibernation for a period. Darrell went to work as a substitute driver for Steve Park in Earnhardt's #1 car, vindicating himself in the eyes of many, with several solid runs in the quality #1 cars. When Park returned from his injuries, Waltrip took over at the #35 team for Todd Bodine and finished the season in the Tabasco-sponsored Pontiacs, but his plans for 1999 were uncertain. One of the cars Darrell ran in 1998 was painted in dedication to driver Tim Flock, who passed away from cancer that year. Waltrip's Tim Flock Special was painted to match the old Carl Kiekhaefer #300 that Flock had driven in the 1950s.

The Independents: The Shift from Drivers to Owners

At the other end of the spectrum from the big-money, multi-car teams are the so-called independents.

Many drivers prefer to concentrate solely on driving and leave the rest of the racing operation to others. There have always been those, however, who have preferred to be their own bosses and run their own race teams. The best-known of these is, of course, Richard Petty Enterprises. Over his long career, Petty drove for another owner in only two seasons, 1984 and 1985, for Mike Curb. Bobby Allison ran his own team whenever he wasn't able to catch a top ride elsewhere.

One of the most independent of the independents is Dave Marcis. Marcis had top-flight seats with the K&K team and with Roger Penske early in his career but returned to his own shop in the late 1970s. He's still driving his signature #71 Chevys today. A plaque in Marcis' shop nicely sums up the spirit of the independent racer: "We've done so much with so little for so long that we can now do anything with nothing."

Although independents are usually considered to be at a disadvantage, there have been some dramatic success stories. Ricky Rudd has been able to continue a sixteen-year winning streak through the last five seasons as owner and driver of the #10 team. And that icon of independence, Alan Kulwicki, earned a Winston Cup championship on his own, after turning down opportunities to drive for the sport's top owners to follow his own dream.

ABOVE: *Ace driver Ricky Rudd left the Rick Hendrick #5 car in 1994 to field his own team. With backing from Tide he attained moderate success, but in 1999 Rudd's fortunes changed. With the loss of his Tide sponsorship in 2000 to a new owner, and after a dismal season in 1999, he sold his team and returned to full-time driving duty with Robert Yates' Texaco #28 car.*
LEFT: *Clad in his familiar Goodyear cap, Dave Marcis is one of the few old-timer independents still able to compete on the Winston Cup circuit.*

Multicar Teams

Multicar teams are certainly nothing new to motorsports; they are common in Formula 1 and Indy racing and have been around in NASCAR since its early days. Carl Kiekhaefer put Mercury Outboard on up to three cars (driven by Buck Baker, Speedy Thompson, and Tim Flock) at once. Though the vehicles weren't exactly part of a team, it seemed like J.D. Stacy was listed as the owner of countless cars in the mid-1980s.

Why do there seem to be so many multicar teams in NASCAR now? There are distinct benefits in running multiple associated teams. As NASCAR competition becomes increasingly intense, teams need as much R&D and testing time as they can get to keep from falling behind. Research is, of course, expensive, and each car is limited (by regulation) in the number of test sessions it can be subjected to in a year. With more cars in a team, the development efforts and testing sessions can be divided up among the cars, and the information shared across the whole team. Thus, a three-car team can learn from three times as many test dates as an independent.

A number of teams have expanded to two-car operations, while others have formed loose associations with competitors to share data. The big names in multicar teams, though, are Hendrick Motorsports, Rousch Racing, and Sabco Racing. Jack Rousch has pushed the limits of the concept—to the point of drawing criticism—with a five-car team. Hendrick is the most successful, dominating the Winston Cup in the second half of the 1990s with four consecutive championships, an unparalleled feat.

OPPOSITE: *Many fans feel that Richard Childress' expansion to a two-car team—he added Mike Skinner's #31 car (seen here trying to find a place in the draft at Daytona in 1999) to Dale Earnhardt's #3 car—contributed to Earnhardt's less-than-dominant performance over the latter part of the 1990s. Most owners, however, feel that multicar teams are no longer an option, but a necessity to remain competitive.*

Perhaps the biggest innovation in 1998 was Ford's introduction of a new model. The company would no longer be producing the trusty Thunderbird, so NASCAR switched to the Taurus. The Taurus, however, is a four-door car, and this aroused skepticism about its eligibility among the GM camp. In addition, the specs and early test models were late getting to many of the teams, so Ford owners felt they were starting the season at a disadvantage, with a largely unknown quantity. Nevertheless, with some midseason rules-tweaking from NASCAR, the Taurus would prove to be a competitive model.

The championship race had a very different complexion in 1998. First of all, everyone was in shock after February, when Dale Earnhardt finally won the Daytona 500. Jaded by previous failures, owner Richard Childress cautioned crew chief Larry McReynolds not to get too excited about Dale leading as he went into the final lap: "We've been here before!" This was the year, though, and Earnhardt filled in that last blank on his astounding stat sheet. Not only did the team win Daytona, but it snapped a long losing streak and restored confidence in Larry McReynolds (who'd been lured to the #3 team from Yates' #28 the previous year). Unfortunately, that was the high point of the season. The team went winless through the rest of the year and fell to eighth in points.

Rusty Wallace was used to starting his season in the points hole, but 1998 was different. It looked like the Taurus might be just the thing to turn Rusty's fortunes around, as he finished second in the first two races and took an early-season points lead. Meanwhile, teammate Jeremy Mayfield astounded everyone with a string of top finishes that put him in second place, right in Rusty's rearview. The two stayed at the head of the points race for the entire first half of the season, with Mayfield leading for much of that time. Mayfield got his first Winston Cup win at Pocono, but immediately fell into a slump that sent him down the standings, to finish in seventh. Wallace continued to be strong for most of the year but just couldn't manage a win. Finally, at the Phoenix race, he broke his losing streak, and finished the season a close fourth in points, behind Dale Jarrett.

The second half of the season belonged to Jeff Gordon, who broke records and tied Petty's modern-era record of thirteen wins in a year. Gordon had to struggle back from an early-season deficit, and it was midsummer before he moved into the points lead. Once there, he never gave it up. The #24 team had hit an autumn slump that endangered the points lead in 1995 and 1997, and actually cost the team the lead in 1996. Gordon had never won a race in October or November. This season was different. The Rainbow Warriors focused and escalated their attack, pulling off three wins in the last four races of the year.

Gordon also made big news with the "No Bull 5" program. He won the Coca-Cola 600 and so was eligible for $1 million at the Brickyard. He won the Brickyard and the million and carried his eligibility to the Southern 500. He won his fourth straight Southern 500—another record—and another million. Dale Jarrett got one of his three wins in the Winston 500, and RJR doled out a third million-dollar payment.

It was the best of times and the worst of times for Rousch's #6 and #99 teams. Jeff Burton won two races, but lost several more to frustrating late-race charges by Gordon. Martin had a dream season of seven wins but couldn't capitalize on them for a title—Gordon was always there ahead of him. At one point, the exasperation in the Rousch garage

Jeff Burton won the inaugural Interstate Batteries 500 at Texas Motor Speedway, and his first Winston Cup race, in 1997. The Exide team, with experienced crew chief Buddy Parrott, was on the verge, with three top-five finishes in the previous four races. They picked up a total of five wins in 1997 and 1998.

bubbled over, with Jack Rousch accusing the #24 team of using special coating on their tires to get their wins. When tires from both teams were tested, no illegal chemicals were found, but it took a while after the "Tiregate" episode for the ill will between the shops to cool.

There weren't many races left after Gordon and Martin were done, but other winners included Bobby Hamilton, in his first year with Larry McClure's #4, and Bobby Labonte, with two wins. Terry Labonte got a win at Richmond with his new crew chief Andy Graves, nudging Dale Jarrett out of the bottom lane on the last lap after leaders Rusty Wallace and Jeff Gordon had wrecked. Rudd won an endurance battle at Martinsville, staying in the car and the lead despite a broken air hose and stifling temperatures. With Earnhardt's winless 1997 season, Rudd became the leader among active drivers for consecutive winning seasons with seventeen—one short of Petty's all-time record.

The Rookie of the Year battle had several solid candidates. Steve Park had the Earnhardt #1 ride, but was injured in a hard crash at Atlanta and missed a number of races. Jerry Nadeau started the season in the Bill Elliott and Dan Marino–owned #13 team, but switched to the #9 car partway through. Kenny Irwin was the eventual Rookie of the Year winner in the Texaco #28.

One of the most familiar sights in Winston Cup racing over the last fifteen years: Dale Earnhardt winning a race. Earnhardt continued to add to his legacy with three wins in 1999 (for a career total of seventy-four). Here he takes the checkered flag at the 1998 Daytona 500, one of the most important victories in his career.

1998 Championship Standings

Place	Car#	Driver	Car Type	Points
1	24	Jeff Gordon	Chevy	5328
2	6	Mark Martin	Ford	4964
3	88	Dale Jarrett	Ford	4619
4	2	Rusty Wallace	Ford	4501
5	99	Jeff Burton	Ford	4415
6	18	Bobby Labonte	Pontiac	4180
7	12	Jeremy Mayfield	Ford	4157
8	3	Dale Earnhardt	Chevy	3928
9	5	Terry Labonte	Chevy	3901
10	4	Bobby Hamilton	Chevy	3786

Special Paint Schemes

As corporate sponsorship became more prevalent in Winston Cup racing, the cars' appearance took on greater importance. The car, and the paint job it displayed, represented the sponsoring company to millions of viewers in the stands and in front of their televisions.

The most famous color in stock car racing is "Petty blue," which originally resulted from Lee Petty stretching a can of blue paint with white to give him enough to cover his car. It is the exception to the rule, as paint schemes became more sophisticated, with colors and decals carefully planned. Artist Sam Bass has made a career not only painting NASCAR celebrities and events but designing dazzling paint schemes for cars. As any NASCAR fan can tell you, there's no richer "eye candy" than a field of forty-two brightly painted cars circling a track on a sunny afternoon or under bright lights at night.

A trend that began in the mid-1990s, and by now has pretty much taken over, is for teams to commission a different paint scheme for their cars to commemorate some special event. While teams often changed the look of their cars from year to year, the use of multiple paint jobs in the same year seemed to really catch on in 1995. That year marked the twenty-fifth anniversary of R.J. Reynolds' involvement with NASCAR—the sponsorship deal was inked in 1970, even

though the first year of the Winston Cup was 1971—and Dale Earnhardt honored RJR with a silver "silver anniversary" car at the Winston Select. That same year, McDonald's used the #94 car to promote its interest in the latest Batman movie, and the #21 Citgo promoted the James Bond *Goldeneye* movie with special cars. The silver Goodwrench and "Thunderbat" cars were immediate hits with fans, who promptly bought up all manner of apparel, collectibles, and toys featuring the unique paint schemes.

That was all it took to open the floodgates. In 1996, not only were the Atlanta Olympic games commemorated by designs on the #3 and #25 cars, but STP's twenty-fifth anniversary with Petty Enterprises was celebrated with a set of five different paint schemes, representing famous Petty cars from the past. Terry Labonte's Kellogg's #5 car gave fans several new looks in his championship season, including the iron gray car honoring him as the "Ironman" of racing (he holds the record for most consecutive races run). One of the most attractive paint schemes (to this writer's eye, anyway) was Rusty Wallace's silver, black, and yellow #2 for Miller Beer's twenty-fifth year in motorsports.

By 1997 and 1998, Winston Cup racing represented a new type of promotional opportunity. Not only were cars painted with the sponsor's colors, but they were serving as rolling bill-

boards that changed from week to week, advertising the latest item in the product line (the #24 DuPont Chromalusion car), division in the corporation (Betty Crocker and Pop Secret on the #26), or box-office release (*Small Soldiers* on the #18 and *The Lost World: Jurassic Park* on the 1997 #24). As automobile-coating technology becomes more and more sophisticated, it wouldn't be surprising if stock cars of the future featured dynamic image panels that changed the cars' appearance and message with each lap.

One of the more intriguing one-off paint jobs had nothing to do with either sponsors or products. In the 1996 Coca-Cola 600, Kyle Petty had been hit with a one-lap black flag penalty for rough driving when he triggered a multicar accident. Owner Felix Sabates complained to the officials that if it had been the #3 car, NASCAR wouldn't have levied the penalty. At the next race, Sabates emphatically made his point by repainting the colorful Coors Pontiac in black and silver—the colors of the #3, making his feelings on the subject of favoritism in NASCAR quite explicit.

ABOVE: *Have a favorite color? Chances are the #9 car was painted with it at some point in the 1998 season. Each paint scheme featured a different set of cartoon characters.*
OPPOSITE: *The #24 DuPont Chromalusion car driven by Jeff Gordon featured a special paint that actually changed colors depending on the angle from which it was viewed.*

1999: A New Champion

The last Winston Cup season of the twentieth century was full of surprises.

For the first time in four years, Hendrick Motorsports did not dominate the season. Terry Labonte won one race at Texas and was a half lap away from winning at Bristol, but otherwise had a mediocre year and finished outside the top ten in the standings. The #25 team never coalesced around Wally Dallenbach and at season's end was ready to try yet another driver next year. The impending loss of well-heeled sponsor Budweiser (which switched to the Dale Earnhardt Jr. team for 2000) likely didn't help.

Jeff Gordon and the Rainbow Warriors were certainly big news throughout the year, but mostly for what they didn't do. First, they didn't finish a handful of races (seven in total). Jeff's seven wins were nothing to scoff at, but were nonetheless a letdown from the success of the previous three years. Their poor fortune (or slightly diminished good fortune), combined with outstanding performances from other top teams, relegated Gordon to sixth in the point standings. They also didn't finish the season with the championship-winning team intact. Rumors were flying through September that Ray Evernham was looking for a new position and would be leaving Hendrick's organization. By the end of the month, Evernham was gone, replaced by crew chief Brian Whitesell. Evernham, Gordon, and Hendrick were mum on the situation until Evernham brought the racing world to its feet with an announcement a couple of weeks later that Gordon had signed a lifetime contract with Hendrick Motorsports.

Also not returning to team #24 were the Rainbow Warriors. Gordon's over-the-wall gang was a professional pit crew—that is, they had no job with the team other than pitting the car on Sundays. As the team defected en masse to Robert Yates' #88 organization, it led to speculation about whether professional crews should be allowed. NASCAR contemplated preventing the trend by limiting the number of team members allowed at the track, but couldn't work out a reasonable approach. Cup teams were pretty well split on whether pro crews should be allowed or not. Given the contribution the crew made to the DuPont team, they'll likely be back in the NASCAR limelight before long.

Evernham was in the spotlight again when he announced that he would be leading Chrysler's return to Winston Cup racing in 2001. After more than twenty years away, Mopar was back. Chrysler talked with various teams about switching to their models, and Evernham planned to return to NASCAR with a team (or two) of his own. At this writing, the make and model of Chrysler car have yet to be determined, though some owners began looking over the Dodge Intrepid as a possibility.

In 1999, for only the third time in the 1990s, there was a new Winston Cup champion. Since his entry into Winston Cup competition in 1984, Dale Jarrett drove for Cale Yarborough, Joe Gibbs, and, most successfully, Robert Yates. The #88 Yates team, with Todd Parrott as crew chief, was a championship contender since it was formed in 1996. With Jarrett fully healthy and Gordon having an off year, the #88 team was able to put all the pieces together in 1999. An extremely popular and well-respected driver, Jarrett is also only the second second-generation driver to win a championship (Ned Jarrett won in 1961 and 1965). And Yates, who has given so much to the sport and gone through so much with his race teams over the years, finally got his well-deserved turn at the top.

Rough and reckless driving was again an issue in 1999, and the usual suspect was at the center of the controversy. Dale Earnhardt showed fans and detractors alike that he was by no means down and out in 1999, winning three races. He swept both Talladega races, dominating the fall race with a victory from the twenty-seventh starting spot—an unparalleled feat on a restrictor-plate track. His third victory was at Bristol, where contact with Terry Labonte on the last lap put the #5 car into the wall, allowing Dale to pass for the win. "Backlash!" read the headlines after the race, and NASCAR deliberated on what action, if any, to take. Earnhardt admitted that he tapped Labonte on purpose, but not with the intention to wreck him. NASCAR elected to take no action and the win stood.

Mike Skinner and Larry McReynolds, at the other RCR team, came close on several occasions to winning their first race. Skinner had two poles, and was the points leader through the first part of the season.

Week after week, rookie contender Tony Stewart wowed the NASCAR community with consistent, top-notch performances in the new Joe Gibbs #20 car. Stewart was not new to racing, but hadn't excelled in the Busch Grand National series the year before, so many observers were waiting for him to falter at the toughest stock car tracks. Well, at the end of the year the skeptics were silenced. Stewart had led more than 1,000 laps, and had thirteen top fives in the year. This included three wins, at Richmond, Phoenix, and the inaugural race at Homestead. He is the only rookie in NASCAR history to win three races in his first season. The team also finished fourth in the points standings, the highest for any rookie driver in Winston Cup history. By all gauges, Stewart had the best rookie season ever in NASCAR. Stewart's teammate at Gibbs Racing was no slouch either. Bobby Labonte put together fives wins and finished second in points. The team was a weekly contender at every track, not just the super-speedways that had been their greatest strength. Labonte proved a master at qualifying as well, with five poles.

The Rousch #6 and #99 teams were again top contenders. Mark Martin picked up two wins despite chronic back problems and a midseason injury and finished third in the points. Jeff Burton had an up-and-down season. The highlights were winning the Winston "No Bull 5" million and six races (second only to Gordon in number of wins).

RIGHT: *At the 1999 K-Mart 400 at Michigan International Speedway, Chad Little (#97), Ted Musgrave (#75), Mike Skinner (#31), and Ricky Rudd (#10), vie for position in a four-wide, perhaps the most dangerous arrangement in superspeedway racing. It was Rudd's last season with Tide sponsorship and Skinner's first as the Intimidator's team-mate.* OPPOSITE: *Dale Jarrett flashes a big smile at the Save-Mart/Kragen 350 in June 1999. Perhaps he knew even then that he was headed for the Winston Cup championship....*

But several poor finishes were enough to keep him out of the top five in the points.

One of the "bad boys" of NASCAR racing hung up his helmet in 1999. Ernie Irvan had had some rough spots in his Winston Cup career, but was undeniably a talented, hard-charging, and popular driver. He had suffered critical injuries in 1994 while vying for the championship and then made an amazing comeback in 1995. After again suffering injuries during a practice run at Michigan (the site of his earlier life-threatening accident), Irvan decided he'd had enough. Ernie retired from the #36 team, and from Winston Cup racing (as a driver). Irvan earned fifteen wins over his thirteen-year career.

Rusty Wallace won early in the year at Bristol, bringing his career wins total to forty-nine. The press made much of the race between him and Gordon to see who could hit fifty first. John Andretti and the #43 team won again at Martinsville in the spring. Another first-time winner in 1999 was Joe Nemechek, former Busch Grand National champion. Joe had earned the nickname "Front Row Joe" for his outstanding qualifying efforts, but had actually been released from his ride at Sabco (Felix Sabates' team) because he hadn't followed through with strong finishes. His dominating win at New Hampshire was the perfect addition to his resumé, and helped him land a spot with Andy Petree's #33 team for 2000.

Notable by his absence in the winner's circle was Ricky Rudd. Rudd had struggled with his team since 1998, and had no opportunities in 1999 to challenge for a win. He had tied Richard Petty's record with at least one win in sixteen consecutive years, but could not break it. Rudd also learned that his longtime sponsor, Tide, would be leaving

him at year's end to sponsor IRL owner Cal Wells' new NASCAR team in 2000. So Rudd decided to get out of the owner/driver business, shutting down his team and signing on to drive for the Texaco #28 team in 2000. Brett Bodine was another owner/driver who sold his team, though remained with the new owners (as had brother Geoffrey the previous year) as driver.

The Winston Cup crowd got a sneak preview of two of the 2000 rookie contenders. Matt Kenseth announced he would drive for a WC team owned by Jack Rousch and Mark Martin, while Dale Earnhardt Jr. signed on with his father, with major sponsorship from Budweiser. Since Kenseth and Earnhardt Jr. had battled closely for the top Busch GN spot in previous years, it was shaping up as a good contest between them for Winston Cup Rookie of the Year honors.

Teams began preparing for the new car models to be released in 2000. Chevy had a new Monte Carlo that received early NASCAR approval. The new Taurus was a bit problematic, and the late nod from NASCAR officials in October didn't give Ford teams much time to prepare for 2000. Ford won the manufacturer's title in 1999 with a solid majority of the wins and won the championship for the first time since 1992.

R.J. Reynolds announced that a fifth race would be added to the Winston "No Bull 5" program—at the three-quarter-mile Richmond track.

On a sad note, the sport bid farewell in November to long-time friend H. Clay Earles. Earles was the owner of Martinsville Speedway, a track that has been part of NASCAR racing since the sport's inception.

Perhaps the most momentous news of the year was NASCAR's new television deal. Up until 1999, each track sold the rights to broadcast its races individually. NASCAR felt that it was necessary to sell coverage as a package and struck a deal with NBC, Fox, and TBS to cover all NASCAR races. The $2.6 billion deal was slated to begin with the 2001 season and last six years. Bill and Brian France described the deal as a defining event in NASCAR's history, one that would bring the sport the same level of coverage and exposure as the NFL and NBA. Racing fans were a bit more skeptical. Most evinced dismay that long-time partners ESPN and ABC were excluded from the deal, and questioned the level and quality of coverage they'd get from the rookie stations. Doubts were fueled by the lackluster coverage in NBC's initial outing, coverage of the Homestead race in November. France has carefully and successfully steered the sport through many rocky shoals over the last twenty-seven years, though, so fans owe him the benefit of the doubt. And no matter what, Winston Cup racing seemed poised to conquer the next millennium.

169

Bibliography

Books

Bongard, Tim, and Bill Coulter. *Richard Petty: The Cars of the King.* Champaign, IL: Sports Publishing, Inc., 1997.

Craft, John. *Classic Stock Cars.* Osceola, WI: Motorbooks International, 1997.

———. *Legends of Stock Car Racing.* Osceola, WI: Motorbooks International, 1995.

———. *Vintage and Historic Stock Cars.* Osceola, WI: Motorbooks International, 1994.

Fielden, Greg. *Forty Years of Stock Car Racing,* vols. 1-4. Surfside Beach, SC: Galfield Press, 1992, 1992, 1989, 1990.

———. *Forty Years of Stock Car Racing Plus Four.* Surfside Beach, SC: Galfield Press, 1994.

Golenbock, Peter. *American Zoom.* New York: Macmillan Publishing, 1993.

———, and Greg Fielden. *The Stock Car Racing Encyclopedia.* New York: Macmillan, 1997.

Holder, Bill. *Stock Car Racing.* New York: Gallery Books, 1990.

Huff, Richard. *Behind the Wall.* Chicago, IL: Bonus Books, Inc., 1997.

Hunter, Don, and Al Pearce. *The Illustrated History of Stock Car Racing.* Osceola, WI: Motorbooks International, 1998.

———, and Ben White. *American Stock Car Racers.* Osceola, WI: Motorbooks International, 1997.

Moriarty, Frank. *The Encyclopedia of Stock Car Racing.* New York: Friedman/Fairfax Publishers, 1998.

Riggs, D. Randy. *Flat-out Racing.* New York: Friedman/Fairfax Publishers, 1995.

Thomy, Al. *Bill Elliott: Fastest Man Alive.* Atlanta, GA: Peachtree Publishers, Ltd., 1988.

Various. *25th Anniversary of Talladega Superspeedway.* Charlotte, NC: UMI Publications, 1994.

Various. *The Darrell Waltrip 25th Anniversary Book.* Charlotte, NC: UMI Publications, Inc., 1997.

Various. *The Life and Times of Harry Gant.* Charlotte, NC: UMI Publications, Inc., 1994.

Various. *NASCAR: The Thunder of America.* Del Mar, CA: Tehabi Books, 1998.

Various. *NASCAR Winston Cup 25th Anniversary.* Charlotte, NC: UMI Publications, Inc., 1995.

Various. *NASCAR Winston Cup Yearbook,* var. eds. Charlotte, NC: UMI Publications, Inc., 1973, 1975–1977, 1979–1985, 1988–1998.

Various. *The Official NASCAR Preview and Press Guide,* var. eds. Charlotte, NC: UMI Publications, Inc., 1991-1998.

Vehorn, Frank. *The Intimidator.* Asheboro, NC: Down Home Press, 1991.

Zeller, Bob. *Mark Martin: Driven to Race.* Phoenix, AZ: David Bull Publishing, 1997.

Periodicals

"98 Faces, the Personalities that Shape NASCAR." *Winston Cup Illustrated,* 1998.

Higgins, Tom. "All in the Family, Part II." *Winston Cup Illustrated,* December 1997.

"Lens Masters." *Winston Cup Illustrated,* March 1996.

Packard, Sam. "Four Days in December." *Winston Cup Illustrated,* February 1998.

Palmer Price, Karsen. "Driver's Good Deeds." *Winston Cup Illustrated,* July 1998.

White, Ben. "Classics: Donnie Allison." *Winston Cup Illustrated,* March 1998.

Appendix

(Note: Current through 1999 season; the term "modern era" denotes the period from 1972 to present)

Championship List

1949 Red Byron
1950 Bill Rexford
1951 Herb Thomas
1952 Tim Flock
1953 Herb Thomas
1954 Lee Petty
1955 Tim Flock
1956–1957 Buck Baker
1958–1959 Lee Petty
1960 Rex White
1961 Ned Jarrett
1962–1963 Joe Weatherly
1964 Richard Petty
1965 Ned Jarrett
1966 David Pearson
1967 Richard Petty
1968–1969 David Pearson
1970 Bobby Isaac
1971–1972 Richard Petty
1973 Benny Parsons
1974–1975 Richard Petty
1976–1978 Cale Yarborough
1979 Richard Petty
1980 Dale Earnahrdt
1981–1982 Darrell Waltrip
1983 Bobby Allison
1984 Terry Labonte
1985 Darrell Waltrip
1986–1987 Dale Earnahrdt
1988 Bill Elliott
1989 Rusty Wallace
1990–1991 Dale Earnahrdt
1992 Alan Kulwicki
1993–1994 Dale Earnahrdt
1995 Jeff Gordon
1996 Terry Labonte
1997–1998 Jeff Gordon
1999 Dale Jarrett

Number of Championships

All-time

Richard Petty	7	Terry Labonte	2
Dale Earnhardt	7	Red Byron	1
Lee Petty	3	Bill Rexford	1
David Pearson	3	Rex White	1
Cale Yarborough	3	Bobby Isaac	1
Darrell Waltrip	3	Benny Parsons	1
Jeff Gordon	3	Bobby Allison	1
Herb Thomas	2	Bill Elliott	1
Buck Baker	2	Rusty Wallace	1
Ned Jarrett	2	Alan Kulwicki	1
Joe Weatherly	2	Dale Jarrett	1

Modern era

Dale Earnhardt	7	Benny Parsons	1
Richard Petty	4	Bobby Allison	1
Cale Yarborough	3	Bill Elliott	1
Darrell Waltrip	3	Rusty Wallace	1
Jeff Gordon	3	Alan Kulwicki	1
Terry Labonte	2	Dale Jarrett	1

Closest Championships

Number of Points	Year	Winner	Runner-Up
10	1992	Alan Kulwiki	Bill Elliott
11	1979	Richard Petty	Darrell Waltrip
12	1989	Rusty Wallace	Dale Earnhardt
19	1980	Dale Earnhardt	Cale Yarborough
24	1988	Bill Elliott	Rusty Wallace
26	1990	Dale Earnhardt	Mark Martin
34	1995	Jeff Gordon	Dale Earnhardt
37	1996	Terry Labonte	Jeff Gordon
47	1983	Bobby Allison	Darrell Waltrip

Manufacturer Wins

Year	AMC	Buick	Chevy	Dodge	Ford	Merc	Olds	Plym	Pont
1972	0	0	10	4	0	0	9	0	8
1973	1	0	7	8	0	11	0	1	0
1974	1	0	12	10	0	7	0	0	0
1975	3	0	6	14	4	3	0	0	0
1976	0	0	13	6	1	10	0	0	0
1977	0	0	21	7	0	2	0	0	0
1978	0	0	10	0	5	4	11	0	0
1979	0	0	18	0	5	3	5	0	0
1980	0	0	22	0	4	2	3	0	0
1981	0	22	1	0	7	0	0	0	1
1982	0	25	3	0	2	0	0	0	0
1983	0	6	15	0	4	0	0	0	5
1984	0	2	21	0	4	0	0	0	3
1985	0	0	14	0	14	0	0	0	0
1986	0	3	18	0	5	0	1	0	2
1987	0	1	15	0	11	0	0	0	2
1988	0	2	8	0	9	0	2	0	8
1989	0	1	13	0	8	0	1	0	6
1990	0	1	13	0	11	0	1	0	3
1991	0	0	11	0	10	0	5	0	3
1992	0	0	8	0	16	0	2	0	3
1993	0	0	8	0	16	0	2	0	3
1994	0	0	11	0	20	0	0	0	0
1995	0	0	21	0	8	0	0	0	2
1996	0	0	17	0	13	0	0	0	1
1997	0	0	11	0	19	0	0	0	2
1998	0	0	16	0	15	0	0	0	2
1999	0	0	12	0	13	0	0	0	9
Total	5	63	356	49	218	51	31	9	63

Owner Wins

All-time		Modern era	
Petty Enterprises	268	Junior Johnson	128
Junior Johnson	140	Rick Hendrick	93
Wood Brothers	97	Richard Childress	67
Rick Hendrick	93	Petty Enterprises	62
Holman-Moody	93	Wood Brothers	59
Richard Childress	67	DiGard	43
Bud Moore	63	Jack Rousch	43
Carl Kiekhaefer	52	Robert Yates	42
Herb Thomas	44	Roger Penske	37
DiGard	43	Harry Melling	34
Nord Krauskopf	43	Harry Ranier	24
Jack Rousch	43	Joe Gibbs	17

Wins from the Pole

Richard Petty	61
David Pearson	57
Darrell Waltrip	24
Bobby Isaac	21
Bobby Allison	20

Superspeedway Wins

Richard Petty	55
Bobby Allison	52
David Pearson	51
Cale Yarborough	50
Dale Earnhardt	47

Most Popular Driver

1956	Curtis Turner
1957	Fireball Roberts
1958	Glen Woods
1959	Junior Johnson
1960	Rex White
1961	Joe Weatherly
1962	Richard Petty
1963	Fred Lorenzen
1964	Richard Petty
1965	Fred Lorenzen
1966	Darel Dieringer
1967	Cale Yarborough
1968	Richard Petty
1969	Bobby Isaac
1970	Richard Petty
1971–1973	Bobby Allison
1974–1978	Richard Petty
1979	David Pearson
1980–1983	Bobby Allison
1984–1988	Bill Elliott
1989–1990	Darrell Waltrip
1991–1998	Bill Elliott

Busch Clash/ Bud Shootout Winners

1979	Buddy Baker
1980	Dale Earnhardt
1981	Darrell Waltrip
1982	Bobby Allison
1983–1984	Neil Bonnett
1985	Terry Labonte
1986	Dale Earnhardt
1987	Bill Elliott
1988	Dale Earnhardt
1989–1990	Ken Schrader
1991	Dale Earnhardt
1992	Geoffrey Bodine
1993	Dale Earnhardt
1994	Jeff Gordon
1995	Dale Earnhardt
1996	Dale Jarrett
1997	Jeff Gordon
1998	Rusty Wallace
1999	Mark Martin

Driver Wins

All-time

Richard Petty	200	Jim Reed	7	Richard Brickhouse	1			
David Pearson	105	Sterling Marlin	6	Dick Brooks	1			
Bobby Allison	84	Dan Gurney	5	Bob Burdick	1			
Darrell Waltrip	84	Alan Kulwicki	5	Marvin Burke	1			
Cale Yarborough	83	Tiny Lund	5	Ward Burton	1			
Dale Earnhardt	74	Dave Marcis	5	Neil Cole	1			
Lee Petty	54	Ralph Moody	5	Jim Cook	1			
Ned Jarrett	50	Lloyd Dane	4	Mark Donohue	1			
Junior Johnson	50	Bob Flock	4	Joe Eubanks	1			
Jeff Gordon	49	Charlie Glotzbach	4	Lou Figaro	1			
Rusty Wallace	49	Eddie Gray	4	Jimmy Florian	1			
Herb Thomas	48	Pete Hamilton	4	Larry Frank	1			
Buck Baker	46	Parnelli Jones	4	Danny Graves	1			
Bill Elliott	40	Herschel McGriff	4	Royce Haggerty	1			
Tim Flock	39	Eddie Pagan	4	Bobby Hillin Jr.	1			
Bobby Isaac	37	Ken Schrader	4	Jim Hurtubise	1			
Fireball Roberts	33	Morgan Shepherd	4	John Kieper	1			
Mark Martin	31	Nelson Stacy	4	Harold Kite	1			
Rex White	28	Billy Wade	4	Paul Lewis	1			
Fred Lorenzen	26	Glen Wood	4	Johnny Mantz	1			
Jim Paschal	25	Bill Blair	3	Jeremy Mayfield	1			
Joe Weatherly	25	Bobby Hamilton	3	Sam McQuagg	1			
Dale Jarrett	22	Dick Linder	3	Lloyd Moore	1			
Terry Labonte	21	Frank Mundy	3	Norm Nelson	1			
Benny Parsons	21	Gwyn Staly	3	Joe Nemechek	1			
Jack Smith	21	Tony Stewart	3	Bill Norton	1			
Ricky Rudd	20	Johnny Beauchamp	2	Phil Parsons	1			
Speedy Thompson	20	John Andretti	2	Dick Passwater	1			
Davey Allison	19	Red Byron	2	Lennie Pond	1			
Buddy Baker	19	Derrike Cope	2	Bill Rexford	1			
Fonty Flock	19	Ray Elder	2	Jody Ridley	1			
Geoffrey Bodine	18	James Hylton	2	Shorty Rollins	1			
Neil Bonnett	18	Bobby Johns	2	Jim Roper	1			
Harry Gant	18	Joe Lee Johnson	2	Earl Ross	1			
Marvin Panch	17	Al Keller	2	John Rostek	1			
Curtis Turner	17	Elmo Langley	2	Johnny Rutherford	1			
Ernie Irvan	15	Danny Letner	2	Greg Sacks	1			
Dick Hutcherson	14	Billy Myers	2	Leon Sales	1			
LeeRoy Yarbrough	14	Jimmy Pardue	2	Frankie Schneider	1			
Dick Rathman	13	Tom Pistone	2	Wendell Scott	1			
Tim Richmond	13	Marvin Porter	2	Buddy Shuman	1			
Jeff Burton	12	Gober Sosebee	2	John Soares	1			
Bobby Labonte	12	Jimmy Spencer	2	Lake Speed	1			
Donnie Allison	10	Emanuel Zervakis	2	Chuck Stevenson	1			
Paul Goldsmith	9	Johnny Allen	1	Donald Thomas	1			
Cotton Owens	9	Bill Amick	1	Tommy Thompson	1			
Bob Welborn	9	Mario Andretti	1	Art Watts	1			
Kyle Petty	8	Earl Balmer	1	Danny Weinberg	1			
Darel Dieringer	7	Brett Bodine	1	Jack White	1			
A.J. Foyt	7	Ron Bouchard	1					

Modern era

Darrell Waltrip	84	Ernie Irvan	15	Jimmy Spencer	2
Richard Petty	81	Tim Richmond	13	Brett Bodine	1
Dale Earnhardt	74	Jeff Burton	12	Ron Bouchard	1
Cale Yarborough	69	Bobby Labonte	12	Dick Brooks	1
Bobby Allison	66	Kyle Petty	8	Ward Burton	1
Jeff Gordon	49	Sterling Marlin	6	Mark Donohue	1
Rusty Wallace	49	Donnie Allison	5	Charlie Glotzbach	1
Bill Elliott	40	Bobby Isaac	5	Pete Hamilton	1
Mark Martin	31	Alan Kulwicki	5	Bobby Hillin Jr.	1
Dale Jarrett	22	A.J. Foyt	4	James Hylton	1
Terry Labonte	21	Ken Schrader	4	Jeremy Mayfield	1
Benny Parsons	21	Morgan Shepherd	4	Joe Nemechek	1
Ricky Rudd	20	Bobby Hamilton	3	Phil Parsons	1
Davey Allison	19	Tony Stewart	3	Lennie Pond	1
Geoffrey Bodine	18	John Andretti	2	Jody Ridley	1
Neil Bonnett	18	Derrike Cope	2	Greg Sacks	1
Harry Gant	18	Ray Elder	2	Lake Speed	1
Buddy Baker	16	Tiny Lund	2		

Winning Percentage (100-race minimum)

All-time		Modern era	
Jeff Gordon	21.5%	David Pearson	22.8%
Herb Thomas	20.9	Jeff Gordon	21.5
Tim Flock	20.8	Cale Yarborough	18.9
David Pearson	18.3	Bobby Allison	13.9
Richard Petty	16.9	Richard Petty	13.1
Fred Lorenzen	16.5	Dale Earnhardt	11.5
Fireball Roberts	16.0	Darrell Waltrip	10.7
Junior Johnson	16.0	Rusty Wallace	9.9
Cale Yarborough	14.8	Davey Allison	9.9
Ned Jarrett	14.2	Tony Stewart	8.8
Dick Hutcherson	13.6	Mark Martin	7.3
Lee Petty	12.6	Tim Richmond	7.0
Fonty Flock	12.3	Bill Elliott	6.7
Bobby Isaac	12.0	Jeff Burton	6.3
Bobby Allison	11.8	Dale Jarrett	5.7
Dale Earnhardt	11.5	Bobby Labonte	5.3
Joe Weatherly	10.9	Neil Bonnett	5.0
Darrell Waltrip	10.7	Ernie Irvan	4.8
Dick Rathman	10.2	Harry Gant	3.8
Rusty Wallace	9.9	Terry Labonte	3.3

Career Earnings

Dale Earnhardt	$35,629,144	Bobby Labonte	12,182,303
Jeff Gordon	27,883,665	Ernie Irvan	11,501,506
Bill Elliott	20,833,223	Kyle Petty	11,341,883
Terry Labonte	20,811,458	Bobby Hamilton	8,670,173
Rusty Wallace	20,332,364	Brett Bodine	8,565,053
Mark Martin	20,392,258	Richard Petty	8,541,218
Dale Jarrett	18,089,901	HarryGant	8,524,844
Darrell Waltrip	18,071,268	Morgan Shepherd	8,402,214
Ricky Rudd	16,611,101	Michael Waltrip	8,217,431
Geoff Bodine	13,964,508	Jimmy Spencer	8,018,611
Ken Schrader	13,586,038	Bobby Allison	7,673,808
Sterling Marlin	13,025,588	Ted Musgrave	7,479,529
Jeff Burton	12,254,225	Rick Mast	6,953,301

Driver Pole Positions

All-time		Modern era	
Richard Petty	126	Darrell Waltrip	59
David Pearson	113	David Pearson	55
Cale Yarborough	70	Cale Yarborough	51
Bobby Allison	59	Bill Elliott	49
Darrell Waltrip	59	Mark Martin	39
Bobby Isaac	50	Geoffrey Bodine	37
Bill Elliott	49	Bobby Allison	36
Junior Johnson	47	Buddy Baker	30
Buck Baker	44	Jeff Gordon	30
Buddy Baker	40	Rusty Wallace	27
Tim Flock	39	Terry Labonte	25
Mark Martin	39	Alan Kulwicki	24
Herb Thomas	38	Ricky Rudd	24
Geoffrey Bodine	37	Richard Petty	23
Rex White	36	Dale Earnhardt	22
Ned Jarrett	35	Ernie Irvan	22
Fireball Roberts	35	Ken Schrader	22
Fonty Flock	33	Neil Bonnett	20
Fred Lorenzen	33	Benny Parsons	19
Jeff Gordon	30	Bobby Labonte	18

The Winston Winners

1985	Darrell Waltrip
1986	Bill Elliott
1987	Dale Earnhardt
1988	Terry Labonte
1989	Rusty Wallace
1990	Dale Earnhardt
1991–1992	Davey Allison
1993	Dale Earnhardt
1994	Geoffrey Bodine
1995	Jeff Gordon
1996	Michael Waltrip
1997	Jeff Gordon
1998	Mark Martin
1999	Terry Labonte

Other Records

Consecutive Seasons

All-time	Richard Petty	35 (1958–1992)
Modern era	Darrell Waltrip	28 (1972–1999)

Consecutive Winning Seasons

All-time	Richard Petty	18 (1960–1977)
Modern era	Ricky Rudd	16 (1983–1998)

Consecutive Races

All-time	Terry Labonte	626 (1979–1999)
Modern era	Terry Labonte	626 (1979–1999)

Consecutive Races Led

All-time	Bobby Allison	39 (1971–1972)
Modern era	Cale Yarborough	25 (1976)
	Darrell Waltrip	25 (1981–1982)

Consecutive Wins

All-time	Richard Petty	10 (1967)
Modern era	Cale Yarborough	4 (1976)
	Darrell Waltrip	4 (1981)
	Dale Earnhardt	4 (1987)
	Harry Gant	4 (1991)
	Bill Elliott	4 (1992)
	Mark Martin	4 (1993)
	Jeff Gordon	4 (1998)

Fastest Race

All-time	Bill Elliott	186.288mph (299.7kph), 1987 Winston 500

Fastest Qualifying Lap

All-time	Bill Elliott	212.809mph (342.4kph), 1987 Winston 500

Numbers of Races, by Track Type

	Short track	Superspeedway	Road course	Total
1949	5	3	0	8
1950	13	6	0	19
1951	33	8	0	41
1952	24	10	0	34
1953	28	9	0	37
1954	27	9	1	37
1955	32	13	0	45
1956	44	11	1	56
1957	42	8	3	53
1958	42	7	2	51
1959	36	8	0	44
1960	30	14	0	44
1961	36	15	1	52
1962	43	10	0	53
1963	42	10	3	55
1964	48	10	4	62
1965	42	11	2	55
1966	35	12	2	49
1967	35	13	1	49
1968	37	11	1	49
1969	37	11	1	54
1970	28	18	1	48
1971	25	21	2	48
1972	9	20	2	31
1973	10	16	2	28
1974	10	18	2	30
1975	10	18	2	30
1976	10	18	2	30
1977	10	18	2	30
1978	10	18	2	30
1979	10	19	2	31
1980	10	19	2	31
1981	10	18	3	31
1982	10	18	2	30
1983	10	18	2	30
1984	10	18	2	30
1985	8	18	2	28
1986	8	18	3	29
1987	8	18	3	29
1988	8	19	2	29
1989	8	19	2	29
1990	8	19	2	29
1991	8	19	2	29
1992	8	19	2	29
1993	8	20	2	30
1994	8	21	2	31
1995	8	21	2	31
1996	8	21	2	31
1997	6	24	2	32
1998	6	25	2	33
1999	6	26	2	34

Index